THE KNOCKNOBBLER

or the Dog-catcher of Worcester

A Diary

BERNARD CARTWRIGHT

Illustrations by Harriet Buckley

PARAPRESS
LIMITED

Also published by Parapress:
Your First Great Dane by Angela Mitchell
Humanity Dick, the Story of Richard Martin, Animal Rights Pioneer
by Peter Phillips

ISBN 978-1-898594-82-6

Illustrations and cover paintings by Harriet Buckley
www.harriart.co.uk

First published in the UK by
PARAPRESS LTD
The Basement
9 Frant Road
Tunbridge Wells
TN2 5SD

www.parapress.co.uk

British Library Cataloguing in Publication Data
A catalogue record of this book is available
from the British Library.

Cover design by Mousemat Design Limited
www.mousematdesign.com

Typeset in Bookman by Parapress Ltd

Printed in Great Britain by Cromwell Press

Print management by Sutherland Eve Production,
Tunbridge Wells, Kent
guy@theeves.fsnet.co.uk

ACKNOWLEDGEMENTS

I would like to thank Anne-Marie (Magie), arch-critic and nit-picker, and the writer Mike Jackson of Severnpix, who set my feet in the right direction; Ms Leslie Gardner of Artellus Limited for her suggestions over the form the book should take and Judith Armstrong for her comments on the text, which were made during a difficult time for her.

I am also indebted to Ken Coombes, Peter Hamblett, Ron Hutchinson, Brian Kent, the inspirational Norah Painter, Peter Sparkes, Natasha Winter, Carole Wood, Subhia Yacoob, the Parapress team and the illustrator Harriet Buckley who so delightfully realised so much about my daily work.

To Magie

CONTENTS

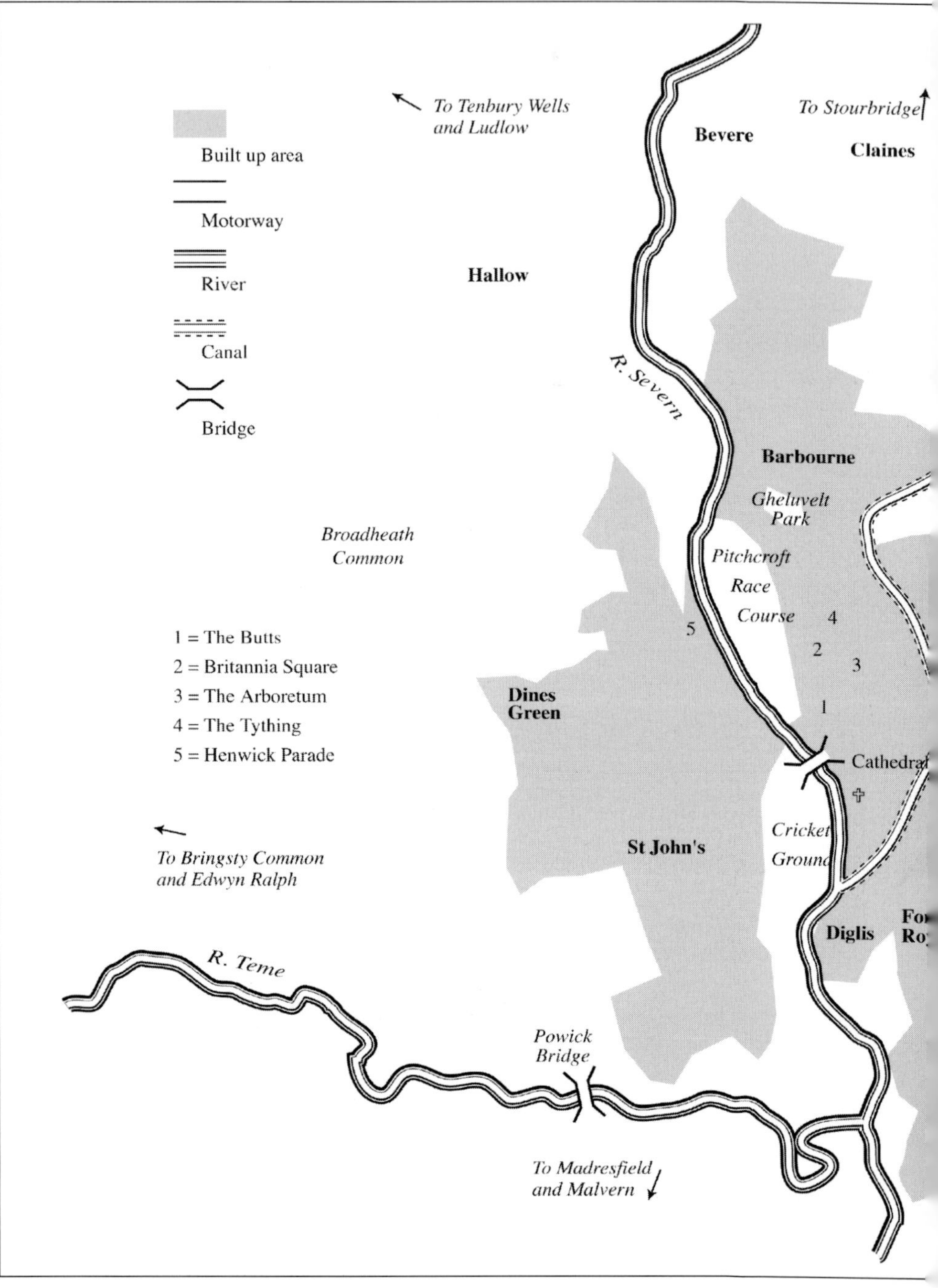

Built up area
Motorway
River
Canal
Bridge
To Tenbury Wells and Ludlow
To Stourbridge
Bevere
Claines
Hallow
R. Severn
Barbourne
Gheluvelt Park
Pitchcroft Race Course
Broadheath Common
1 = The Butts
2 = Britannia Square
3 = The Arboretum
4 = The Tything
5 = Henwick Parade
5
4
2
3
1
Dines Green
St John's
Cathedral
Cricket Ground
To Bringsty Common and Edwyn Ralph
Diglis
Fo Ro
R. Teme
Powick Bridge
To Madresfield and Malvern

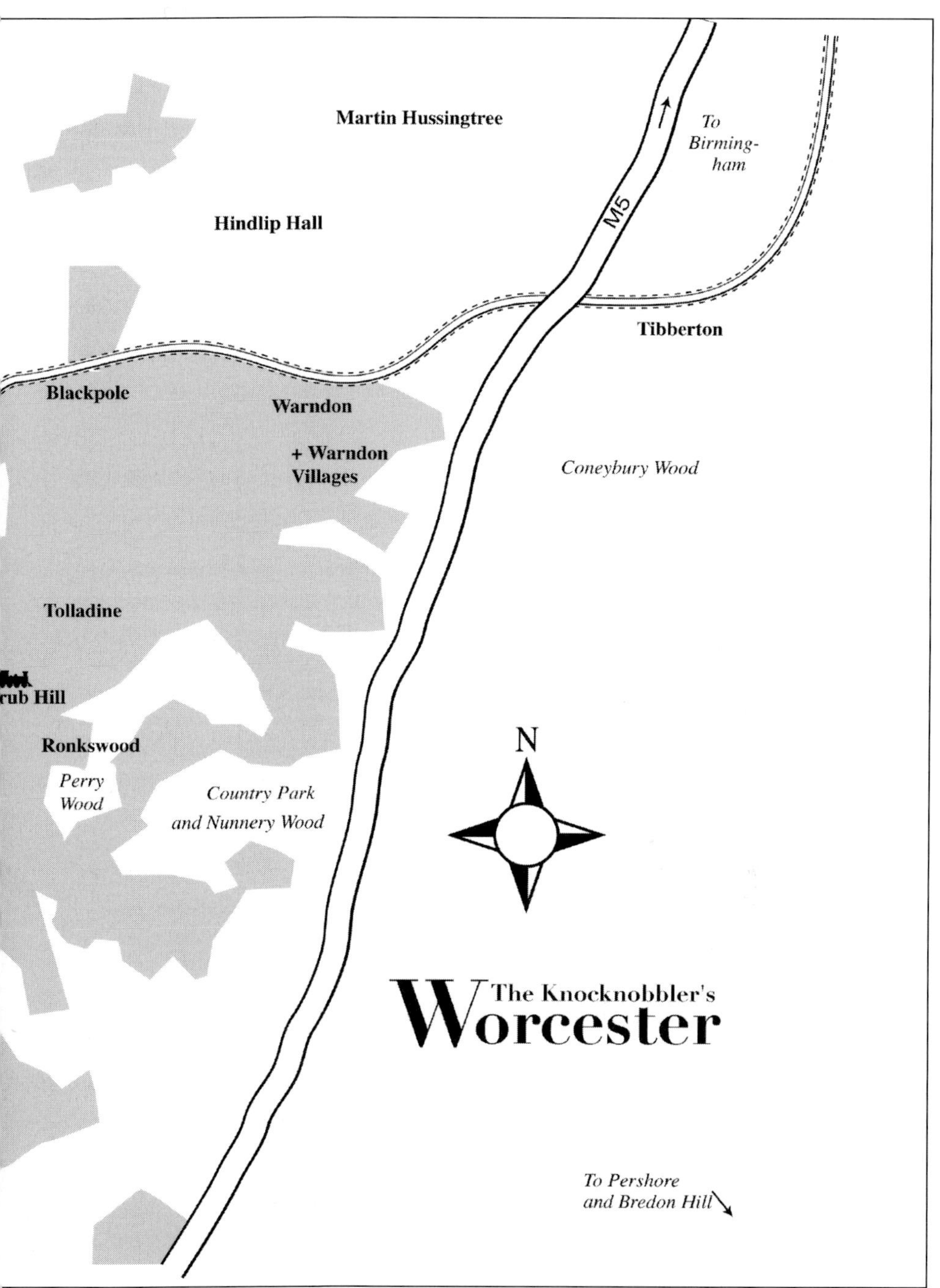

Martin Hussingtree
To Birming- ham
M5
Hindlip Hall
Tibberton
Blackpole
Warndon
+ Warndon Villages
Coneybury Wood
Tolladine
rub Hill
Ronkswood
Perry Wood
Country Park and Nunnery Wood
N
The Knocknobbler's
Worcester
To Pershore and Bredon Hill

Yᵉ Knocknobbler.

A knocknobbler:

an ancient term for the person engaged by a church to eject unruly dogs from acts of worship.

AUTHOR'S NOTE

This diary was drafted in the field, sometimes literally. I wrote it on the streets of Worcester and in the villages around, often seated in uncomfortable postures and sometimes scribbling on wet paper. I was not, initially at least, seated at a word processor or drooling over long cups of coffee. I wrote it long-hand into notebooks, and on scraps of paper after frantically looking for a biro, and often by the light of a torch on wintry days.

While telling the story of a three-year quest, it focuses on farcical doggie episodes and the minutiae of canine life, which are naturally linked with the foibles of Worcester's dog owners. These daily events were often laughed over, across our family table.

Some of the incidents have been changed, for two reasons: firstly to save the red of embarrassment from covering the faces of Worcester's dogs, on account of the antics of their owners. Secondly, and mainly in profound sympathy with man's best friends which are so often called by amusing names like Lenin or Kiki-Babe, I have been moved to turn the tables and give the dogs their sweetest revenge ever, by re-naming their proprietors.

Making people laugh was one of my intentions. Just as fireworks are composed of elements from the earth below which when compressed together can be ignited, illuminating the darkness above, so my two related themes of work and belief, when mixed with the dogs will, I hope, burst into humour.

I had at first intended the text to be purely observational, akin to my television documentary film-making experiences, and to allow the dogs and people of Worcester to 'speak' for themselves. However, to omit myself would have been to gloss over my thoughts and preoccupations whilst I worked. So I have let in my personal take on life, which journeys into some other worlds with other leitmotivs, such as that of the Byronic outsider! far removed from the animals. These reflections were written after some incident or catalyst pulled me up short during the vagaries of the working day, and were buffed up later.

While my journal is essentially like a puppy's playful quest, it sadly also contains references to animal cruelty and violence as I encountered them and reflects how I was fiercely moved. This diary has had a life all of its own. I guided its teetering steps, but I didn't know how it would evolve or indeed end.

PART ONE

Be convinced that there are other and better things even in this life

I am his Highness's dog at Kew,
Pray tell me sir, whose dog are you?
Alexander Pope - on the collar of a dog he gave to his Royal Highness.

Monday 6th September 1999

The Venice lagoon sometimes freezes over in winter. Magie and I stood in the wintry sunset admiring two cities for the price of one, by reviewing Venice's diffused reflection in the wafer-thin ice, the scene which artists yearn for. Our vantage point was the Island of Saint Lazarus, the location of a monastic community, the Congregazione Armena Mechitarista.

I remembered this (oh so well) today, as I slowly slipped on, for the first time, my dark blue rubbery uniform as the Dog Catcher for Worcester City.

Behind me on that Venetian island, just by the jetty, was an inscription attributed to Lord Byron, who once had a study in the monastery: 'Be convinced that there are other and better things even in this life.'

Today I wondered how I could possibly go forward to those elusive 'better things' dressed up as I was?

I had been at the Venice Carnival with Magie my wife and her sister Claire Bretécher the famous French cartoonist and enlivener of the human spirit, together with her genial husband Professor Guy Carcassonne of the University of Nanterre in Paris, the world authority on the French Constitution.

This break followed my redundancy from Central Independent Television in 1991. I was one of the 'Birmingham Six Hundred' whose careers were stymied by that insane battle to keep the Midlands ITV franchise, fought between people who wanted to trouser even more money while still retaining, famously, a licence to print it. They effectively ended the Renaissance of British broadcasting, whilst introducing a new phrase to the English lexicon - 'dumbing down'.

Before working with the dogs I had made 200 job applications, those brimming repositories of fleeting hopes which become mausoleums of coloured paper clips and A4 paper. Shortly after 'leaving' Central ITV I was turned down for a job at GCHQ in Cheltenham on the stated grounds of my French connection. Apparently we are still at war with Napoleon.

Well, these are reduced circumstances: going from working in television as a cameraman, researcher and finally as a director to ending up being a Dog Catcher; but they should hold no terrors for me. No work or dole should be perceived as degrading but, yes, unemployment itself puts the bite into a family like nothing else save divorce or death.

Thus, then, I reflected on my previous good fortunes. I forgave those who turned me into a 'jobber,' for if I did not, they would still continue to have power over me. 'Yet what deep wounds ever closed without a scar?' (Byron)

I wonder today what Providence holds for our family?

Thursday 9th September 1999

Many people are going to the dogs but few, like me, have actually arrived! After only three days' pupilage I am now out on my own, joining that honourable corps of civic servants which includes the Rat Catcher, the Gravedigger and the Public De-Louser.

I feel mightily incapable of restraining dangerous dogs and vicious people, of issuing fines for strays and prosecuting the public under the Fouling of Land Act 1996 (Dogs). How, too, am I to manage millions of seconds of boredom?

I am instructed that Worcester City Council is not a dog welfare organisation and that stray cuddly dogs must be considered, from the ratepayer's perspective, as public nuisances plain and simple.

To help me along, I have been given a policeman's blue 'time' book, making me an arbiter of admonishments, reproofs, reprimands, final warnings, cautions and even convictions. (As you will see, the indignant 'gorblimey guvs' in the populace perceived these as a medley of encroachments into their personal liberties, and people like me as a civic intrusion.)

I have been given a van, 'Pixie', for picking up strays, together with all the paraphernalia for dog catching, redolent of the Disney cartoon *Lady and the Tramp*. In fact the vehicle has every requisite to deal with dogs, except a grooming parlour, a Kalashnikov and number plates reading K9 JAIL. I am also responsible for an expensive pair of 'oglers', (binoculars) and am duly licensed to spy on women whilst getting paid for it, solely in respect of their dogs' fouling, of course.

My first phone call informed me of a roaming Alsatian with an interest in a butcher's shop in the long, narrow, twisting street called Lowesmoor. I parked on yellow lines with my yellow light whirling round as if intending to give bystanders an epileptic fit. It transpired that the dog owner was actually inside the shop but, before I could call her out, a tramp, looking like a member of Fagin's gang, stepped forward and approached the black-and-tan Alsatian. The young dog retreated arsy-versy along the crowded pavement but the man followed it, just managing to loop the belt from his trousers around its neck whilst declaring to me, 'I'm Nero Carstairs, me boy, I often help people like you stuck with dogs!'

With much palaver this gentleman promenaded across Lowesmoor towards Pixie in a parody of a dog-catcher. I stopped him just in time because the owner of the dog came out from the butcher's shop. On appraising the gridlocked traffic and the mêlée, this lady breathed, 'Phew!' and uttered profound apologies all round, her face going cherry red like a blacksmith's steel as she gratefully received her dog back.

Mr Carstairs, still eager to be a part of the action, expressed the jollyism: 'We folk don't mind helping your sort out, but I risk charges for indecent exposure if I don't get me belt back!' ... Worcester sauce!

Later this first morning after an 11am brekkie, I patrolled the Barbourne district of the city, which has a prominent bridal shop, Gatehouse Brides, whose tastefully presented silks seem to waft jaded motorists and bleary-eyed lorry drivers along the main road into The Tything, and to work. Just past Gheluvelt Park, almost opposite the shop, a chic young lady threw herself across the bonnet of my moving Pixie in a welter of self-denunciation akin to those which prisoners of Chairman Mao were coerced into. Seemingly, Mrs Ginny Sloe's two Cavalier King Charles Spaniels had got out and she thought I was on my way to catch them and carry them off to Council kennels or worse, but I knew nothing about them except that, Worcester being a Royalist stronghold, this sort of dog is everywhere.

A fine lady this, humble, apologetic and very bright, and so I wonder whether she was the prototypical voter 'Worcester Woman,' wooed by the Labour Party, like others before her such as 'Essex Woman' and 'Mondeo Man' previously cultivated by the Tories. It

was during the 1997 General Election that Tony Blair and his team was said to have targeted 'Worcester Woman'. Perhaps I should use some of my 'seconds of boredom' to try and discover her, keeping the details of this quest in a diary of associated events. This seems to me a most delectable prospect!

Arrived home reeking. Tonight Schtroumpf,* our Border Collie, rose up from our doormat to sniff the new doggy smells from my trousers. When she laughs, a centimetre of skin in each corner of her mouth forms a smile and today it was a full one. Who says dogs don't have a sense of humour? 'Tis sweet to know there is an eye will mark our coming ... and look brighter when we come.' (Byron, *Don Juan*, on the honest watchdog.)

* Phonetically sounding like the German for 'sock' as well as being a cartoon character.

Tuesday 14th September 1999

Responded to an incident in which common sense seemed as rare as horse muck under a rocking horse.

I attended a home in Georgian inner Worcester, to visit the pettifoggers who had complained about a lady in a wheelchair who doesn't clean up after her guide dog, if you can credit it. I noted the shimmering deposit in question. Now the problem was that the wheels of the wheelchair get stuck in the lawns, making mobility a problem, though the lady told me she has permission to 'let her dog piss under Gordon's tree', which is accessed by a path.

She told me she was injured in a car accident whilst working as a nurse in New York. She was terribly sweet and feminine, in a horsey way, yet flinty enough to threaten to dump horse manure (not covered by dog fouling law) outside her neighbour's property as an act of revenge for narking on her.

I gave the complainants diplomatic short shrift, with a hint that they could help by picking it up themselves. I resolved to supply this handicapped lady with 'Worthybag' Council poop kits evermore and definitely gave her the second entry in my Worcester Woman diary. However, as I left the location, I was approached by another irate resident, Kurt McTrudgett:

"Ere, 'ave you told that "raspberry ripple" [cripple] to stop arsing up our lawns?' Uncommon parlance for Georgian Worcester and no illustration of the spontaneous generosity of the human spirit.

'Sir, sir!' I replied, 'It is private property here, so you'll have to deal with it yourself, but I have had a quiet word, yes.'

I was told, 'You people from the Council do nothing except pick up the Poll Tax.' The dignity of my municipal position meant I could not give utterance to my sentiments.

Relief and lunch in the Cathedral Cloister café, the finest works canteen and ecclesiastical salon in the world, to trough myself on fruit cakes and coffee.

Roy Fidoe (sic) my City Council boss, Head of Dog Services and Environmental Health, grumbled about me taking his parking place at our Farrier House office. But Roy is a Brummie whose kindness is only exceeded by his zeal for the people of Worcester. He is a fellow who has struggled to reject the vanities of public office and not a management careerist who treads on a few necks and then moves on, unless of course someone attempted to stamp on his neck first. It was Roy who jestingly gave me the dubious sobriquet 'St Bernard' which stuck around the office for a bit. Nevertheless, Pixie is an operational dog van whereas his car is a rather sterile occupant of this particular piece of council tarmac.

Wednesday 15th September 1999

The Story of Emily

What I had to do today would send a teenager's stomach muscles into spasm with ribald laughter: I had to caution a policeman!

A Post Office manager sent me a report about an attack upon one of his staff by a police dog at the officer's home. I read the postman's statement in which he claimed the Alsatian had jumped on his shoulders from the rear, a truly terrifying experience.

I first met the wife of Police Constable Rong I-Ul-Haqit in their doorway; she had to stop the wayward dog, possibly a trainee, running up the wall before she could speak to me. 'He's not always like this,' she protested and then went on to admit the bald facts of the attack.

I then spoke to the police officer and formally warned him that he had a special duty to keep a police dog like his in order at all times. He made an apology which was neither too servile nor too surly, adding apprehensively, 'You are not going to take this matter any further are you?' I deemed that having to receive a caution from a civilian was sufficient punishment and reassured him I would not. The police have enough grief without me adding to it and most police dog handlers love their dogs to bits as family pets; besides I didn't want to prejudice my supply of coffee and welcome sit-down behind the front desk at Worcester police station.

Two days later I had to enforce the provisions of PIDDLE, the 1998 Public Interest (Dogs) Disclosure Legislation.* This took precedence over the European Human Rights protocols regarding intrusive surveillance, since the subject being watched was not human. So I was on patrol outside the policeman's house to ensure that a possible dog attack was not part or parcel of this postman's lot, when my phone burst into life with the report of a dog attack on yet another postman.

I peeled off and drove to the location of this new incident, first going via the office to check with Kate the name of the dog owner in the electoral register. Ten minutes later I was climbing the steps to the imposing front door of Mrs Emily Wantuch, having first rattled the gate to see if there was a raging dog in the garden.

* Bernard's imagination is at work here - Ed.

The occupier opened her front door gently, as if folding over a leaf of a tasteful version of the Pirelli tyre calendar. There stood a large black poodle whose dreadlocks covered its brows, making it appear eyeless. Next to the dog was a tall lady wreathed in a loose black dressing-gown, with long panther-black tousled hair fresh from the shower resting on her shoulders.

'Oh no! you haven't come for Tosca have you? Look, you can see she really is tame, aren't you Tosca?'

'Look, madam .... '

'Please please don't take her away; she won't do it again!' Tosca started to whine at her owner's distress.

I said: 'Can't you keep her in at 8 o'clock when the postman calls?'

'I will, I will, of course I can, yes!'

'Perhaps you can put her in the back garden instead of the front if she needs to go out.'

'Yes, yes I will.'

'You see, madam, we can't have a large dog like this bearing down on members of the public utilities who have the right of access to your front door.'

Composing herself, Emily replied, 'No of course not, please come in,' and I followed her warm moist footmarks across the cool Meissen tiled hall and into her lounge.

I noticed a painting from South America on the wall and remarked on it. Tosca's owner replied, 'It's the La Limonada shanty of Guatemala City, I worked as an accountant for a coffee firm in London and we commissioned a series of paintings on South and Central America for the boardroom. I actually visited Guatemala: it was all filth and corruption.'

'Just like Worcester,' I added, and I'd broken the ice by doing so.

Her lounge looked as if hermetically sealed against children. On the mantelpiece sat an old working clock with the letters VR on the face. Tucked in behind it was a brochure for a weekend tour of the Clement something-or-other library in Prague. On the other side of the clock were some boxes of medication, one marked 'Diazepam' (trade name for Valium). A Steinway concert grand piano arrayed in antique silver, every piece seemingly knowing its place, dominated the room and a CD was gently purring with Vivaldi. The piano stool was stacked with Yoga cards, the top one illustrating the sun salutation posture. Tosca the poodle fitted in here perfectly, being a breed which sheds very little hair.

Emily invited me to sit at one end of a Chesterfield sofa while she and Tosca ensconced themselves at the other. 'Don't you think that Vivaldi just transports you to each of the Four Seasons? Would you like a cigarette?'

'No thank you, I don't take the weed.'

'Look I'm really sorry about the dog, the rear garden is just a patio, that's all, so she has to "go" in the front.'

'Could you put a letterbox at the garden gate?'

'No! Roddy, my husband, works for Strunk's Kettles and Holloware up in Lye so we would need a letterbox as big as a shed for all the samples and mail he receives. He owns the company actually. Your Postman, the moron, kicked over my flower pots in a fit of pique, you know; all Tosca wanted to do was nuzzle up to the fool, that's all. She's a poodle, not a guard dog.'

'That's not how the postman sees it; the dog is calm now because she is with you.'

Emily rose from the sofa, went over to the CD player and shut the music off; padding back barefoot to the mirror over the fireplace she stood there a while, then proceeded to look at me in reflection. 'I'm a farm secretary near Broadheath, part-time that is; I suppose I could give Tosca some more exercise out there. When Roddy gets home all he wants to do is sit in a chair, he cares nothing for Tosca.'

She looked fleetingly in the mirror at herself and then back at me adding, 'Roddy's got other passions and I'm not one of them.' She started to light up a Black Russian type cigarette, then after busying herself with the packet and the lighter she made a wink at me. 'If Roddy tumbled into a barrel of bosoms he would come out sucking his thumb.'

Following a pause, she then informed me in the weaselly cadence of an anticipated sexual fumble, 'He's not in today.'

'Can we talk about the matter in hand Mrs Wantuch?'

Turning to face me she said, 'I like being given instructions by a firm man! Would you like some of the "wacky baccy" - cannabis I mean? - I get it off somebody who uses it for MS.'

'Look, I said I don't smoke.'

'I can do you a cocktail mix of Valium and cider.' After a displeased fidget at my facial response, Emily puffed her cigarette and simmered, 'If only you knew how I felt you wouldn't treat me so lightly.' She then picked up her hand-bag from the mantelpiece and threw it down beside me on the sofa. 'Look in there, look and you will find a reason to stay,' she said enticingly.

I didn't care even to look at the bag let alone open it, but thought to myself, 'Why do people have to endure the frustrations they are least able to cope with?' I then spoke softly: 'Emily, I sense you are a person with very deep needs but I don't have the inner resources to respond to your problems. Why don't you talk it over with someone who can give you some help and direction for all of this, ... this ....' I was on the move, followed by the patter of six feet coming after me down the hall. I descended the steps rapidly with Tosca bounding alongside me yelping with delight. When I reached the gate I turned and saw Emily slouching against the door jamb; she shouted, 'What do you think I am, some sort of whore out from Walsall working the shires? Goodbye!'

I took a needed tea break from the encounter with Emily and travelled for my relief to Old Northwick river meadows, which are within the city limits. White-rumped Martins were congregating for their trip to Africa. The birds flitted across the Severn's swirls like snow flakes performing to the notes of Elgar's Cello Concerto. Three boys were fishing and I guess singing to themselves the Worcester fisherman's song:

Pike, perch, bream, eel and tench,
No more sitting on the old school bench.

It was here that young Elgar, at the same age as these kids, used to sit and compose 'What the reeds are singing'... .

About two years later I was watching the obedience trials of the dog training club on the Countryside Park, as I did most Thursday lunchtimes, when the red shale of the car park was torn up by Emily's 'Chelsea Tractor,' a Land Rover Freelander 4x4, (well, Emily does work on a farm). She got out of her vehicle and into a Renault Espace driven by a middle-aged man who similarly tore up the car park in a bull-at-a-gate manoeuvre to get away. As they blasted off I wondered whose marriage she was ruining today and if she ever took up my suggestion of seeking help (apparently not). Over my sandwiches I considered that, while the human body is hewn for love, (especially Emily's), the illusory pillow of adultery is not just forbidden for the sake of it, it is forbidden because it ultimately, like the Freelander, cuts everything up.

I sauntered over to her vehicle and there was the giant poodle on the back seat. I noticed that despite her turmoil Emily had remembered to leave the car windows slightly open so that at least Tosca could breathe and not perish in the heat.

Monday 20th September 1999

First sad and bad case.

There I was, sitting in the van, relaxed and watching the clouds weighing themselves on the top of Bredon Hill like cotton wool wadding on burnished Salter scales. Then the emergency call comes.

A quick drive back through the delicate undulating geometry of Archers' country eventually brought me to a location at the rear of Worcester Cathedral, where an old white Terrier bitch, tied up with baling twine, was abandoned, like a leper at a monastery gate. The dog had no traceable collar tag or micro-chip ID. There was less meat on the poor creature than on a butcher's pencil and her nether parts were shot through with mammary cancer. Her weight in my arms was as nothing.

The experience reminded me keenly of the time when, filming Mother Teresa of Calcutta, I had held her grey cardigan, which was unexpectedly as light as tissue paper because it had been washed so many times in her Home for Dying Destitutes.

I suspected that, during the eight days we normally keep a dog before it is put up for re-homing, no visitor would stoop to pick up this emaciated pet from off the floor.

When I arrived at our Burdock-juxta-Bredon Council kennels, Sue, who was in charge, cut up rough over the cruel owner, the author of this obscenity. I then drove to a vet's with Sadie, a kennel maid, who was distraught over the appalling state of the Terrier.

During my pedal-to-the-metal drive to a Droitwich Spa veterinary surgery, life was ebbing away from the dog like stuffing from a hugged comforter cushion. Poor Sadie gave the skeletal animal as much solace as she could in her tender hands; making its tail wag happily for the last time prior to letting me place it on the table for the lethal injection. Within three seconds the dog had succumbed. We drove back in tears: Sadie cried out, but I wept interiorly.

Tuesday 21st September 1999

Let us call him Zorba Athalos, my subject for today.

I was on poowatch, inspecting a dirty footpath leading from a housing estate into woodland and had found eight sets of faeces, when a wizened man of Greek extraction appeared unbidden at my side, offering the following advice about the mess alongside his property.

'You wana dee fiery coal poka upa dee arse of dee dorgs and upa dee ownas, liker dee steel upa dee Boches' arse. People ere am dee pig swill and nota know eet. Hevery 'ouse 'ere 'as noosance of a dorg. Many dorgs ina dee street foula alladee night lorng. You tella ownas and eet lieek dee piss in dee wind. Sorry I er do not speeka bitter English.'

He was the most troubled foulee I ever met in Worcester, and I recruited him immediately into my 'listening post' team of dog spies.

Worcester is made for romanticism. The fresher to this city doesn't have to struggle to seek out its delights: he is in their midst. Midst is a very rich and special word for me. In Worcester you are in the midst of beauty, and you cannot fail to observe the city's gentility. Though I patrol Britannia Square, for example, I do not so much patrol it as receive an impulse to convey Pixie there to imbibe its healing Georgian homes and gardens. It is spatially more accessible and less constricted than the Regent's Park terraces or even the centres of Oxford or Paris in all their magnificence.

Britannia Square contains the scruffy vitality of children's delights casually strewn in front gardens, and of dustbin bags resonating in the breeze. It provides, in contrast with some provincial cities, a picturesque answer to the problems of existing cheek by jowl. Similarly, the Worcestershire villages are without equal except perhaps in Tuscany or Provence. Sussex and Kent, for example, are just too tidied up.

The well matured red of the city's brickwork even seems more tasteful than the smoked yellow of London's brick. Worcester buildings make you cheerfully good tempered, just as the light from the magnificent Hardman Creation window in the Cathedral seems to mellow presenting hardships, while the modern Pieta in St Wulfstan's crypt can unsettle your settled resentments. The Cathedral itself stands as a witness against exuberant secularism, and even seen in the stirred cappuccino of its own reflection in the muddy Severn, gives a sense of steadfastness in the midst of the swirls and caprices of this life. Like its Cavalier Spaniels, the 'Faithful City' can also present an aloof air.

One street wit on the London Road, whose Black Labrador was called Humph - known down the hill in Sidbury as 'the humph' because of its habit of trying to tango with the traffic – gave me a kerbside seminar just after I'd cautioned him over his dog's habitual roaming.

As we both had time to spare, we started up a conversation. Mr Jeremy Trillington, a walking plea for the exigencies of commerce, mentioned he'd recently retired from the London Metal Exchange, so we easily struck up a conversation about the demise of the traditional 'metal bashing' industries in the Black Country.

I said, 'When I was a boy you could go the end of the garden and whistle into any factory yard and someone would come out and offer you a job. Today the old industries are being allowed to run down as part of a deliberate economic policy, yet we still need steel and cars.'

He replied, 'If you were right I would go along with you! We can't compete with factories in China and India where whole families consider it an honour to live on the premises and where their industry is actually nurtured by their banks. They can dump their products on the wharf at Southampton cheaper than we can make them. The Black Country failed to innovate. If we went along with all the squealing and industrial philosophy from up there we would still have a foundry in Worcester making cannon balls to fight Cromwell!'

When I had hoisted myself up onto his mental level I replied, 'It's not that simple: if we had put a stop to the stalking of our manufacturing industry by the Japanese, in the same way as the French protected their electronics industry by specifying a single point of entry for Japanese electronic products at an obscure airfield supervised by two dawdling officials, there would not have been so much unemployment in the Black Country.'

I then threatened to deprive Mr Trillington of his cash for allowing his Labrador to stray, which concentrated his mind somewhat.

A kindly old Worcester acquaintance of mine, whose charity remains hidden, was prepared to sink his personal pension into his Black Country factory to purchase another month's wages for his staff ... . Greater love has no one than this, that he lays down his wallet for his friends.

Thursday 23rd September 1999

Give a dog a bad name . . .

To Binx Bros Engineering, where the manager had complained about a stray mongrel getting into the premises.

At the side of the factory I found the dog happily nosing among the rose-bay willow herb and moist moss-covered pallets which dwelt there. It was so spooked it became uncatchable. After ten minutes I backed off to let it wander home, with me following it in order to meet its owner. The mongrel jumped down a bank of industrial scree into the putrid backyard of Mrs

Basilia Bultitude, and I scrambled down the bank too, (perilous at 54). The mongrel joined two other blighted dogs, and yapping started up. I called to the lady, who came out of her kitchen, responding 'What the f****** hell's the matter?'

There is always something of interest in a human face and although this one might have been pulped in a pub brawl many a time, her eyes were compassionate. I wondered if this was the real Worcester Woman. I tactfully explained that her dog was out and might get run over, additionally reminding her that the adjacent factory housed dangerous chemicals.

She said, 'I'm all on me own here and the b****** Council refuse to fix the fences, what can I do about it?'

I jettisoned the formal 'Madam' for the warmer 'Love' in my mode of address. 'Look, love, you are responsible for your pet.' She replied: 'It's them in the bleedin' factory which feeds me dogs, they ought to be payin' me for providin' guard dogs for them but they oodn't give yer the sparks off their grinder! Why don't they go and piss in someone else's hat?'

As Basilia held forth in her stark kitchen, I felt I was being kippered by her tobacco smoke. Yet I noticed from her features a quality within, which seemed never to have been called forth from her. The good inside her was guttering away in foul language. No doubt the world would tend to answer this lady's problems with a blow or letters printed in red ink deposited on her doormat. Encounters with people like Basilia disposes my biro to squiggle red ink too, but with indignation on their behalf.

Though later I did enter her in my 'red book' which listed canine nuisances and people to be watched, the reality of my feelings was warmer. Subsequently the factory was to build its own fence, but I kept a friendly eye on that particular road for her stray mongrels, as I have always been a sucker for 'outsiders' and those devoid of self-friendship.

I bumped into Nero Carstairs again and, blimey! he was not a tramp after all but a winsome man living on Rainbow Hill! He looked dishevelled but didn't have an unkempt nature, in fact the very opposite. He had the sweetest little rusty-haired collie with a nose as shiny as a recruiting sergeant's boots pacing through the dew. Nero spent his days sauntering around Worcester really trying to do good to people. How wrong could I be? I recruited him immediately into my dog spy network and his top grade information enabled me to run to earth several early morning filth merchants in the Tolladine and Rainbow Hill districts.

Pulled up behind a Volvo estate car at the lights next to the Commandery Civil War Museum. The vehicle's sticker read :

KEEP CATS
DOGS 0 – THE THROAT IN 0.1 SEC.

Saturday 25th September 1999

On a welcome day off, free from the smells of Pixie, I went to the Birmingham Oratory Church for a training day with Crux, an organization for lay Roman Catholics active in the social milieu.
 I was proud to associate again with people like Brian Carey, whose faith was as strong as a granite calvary and who as a young man used to sell *The Universe*, a Roman Catholic paper, outside tube stations next to the Communist *Daily Worker* stand, like a modern Saint Paul preaching against the pagans. Unfortunately, too many Roman Catholics are insensible to the need for this kind of social action and prefer instead a moderate and non-combatant stoicism. It was Graham Greene, I think, who once said that 'Roman Catholics are meant to be revolutionaries but end up being eccentrics.'

About a month into the job, and time to take stock.

If men were made 'a little lower than the angels' but higher than the brute beasts, dog catchers were made a little lower than policemen but slightly higher than the canines whose antics they are trying to curtail. The key words in the job description would be Roaming, Howling, Fouling and Growling. As I now see it, really to get the best results for the public there needs to be a government regulatory body called Ofdog, which has the necessary expedients to superintend the whole of the canine world.
 Most days see me patrolling the streets, answering distress calls on either my phone or my two-way radio, with its call sign

of Delta Whisky (Dog Warden). I try to be a presence rather than a dog policeman and to encourage people to find their own solution to a dog problem. I like this job and its invigorating physical freedom. Not many people get paid for walking the Severn. The task of being on the trail of Worcester Woman is especially fulfilling! During the working day I tend to see more women than men anyway.

This taking stock occurred while out with my whirligig of loyalty and mischief, Miss Schtroumpf, as we walked together in Oldswinford Churchyard, Stourbridge. The relief of its weathered headstones resembles that of ancient standing stones of Carnac in Brittany. I go there to read these gravestones, an odd form of relaxation but it works for me.

In fact, the ancient records of St Mary's Church indicate that in the 1600s the Church Wardens engaged an assistant dog catcher called a Knocknobbler, sometimes known as the Dog Whipper or the Sluggard Walker.* This person's task was to eject nuisance dogs, often belonging to shepherds, from acts of worship by using a large pair of wooden or iron dog tongs as a grasper, not really a bad tool at all. Giant tongs like these would solve many of my dog-catching problems. Sometimes I wish I could have been a no-nonsense Dog Catcher like that.

The other tasks of a Knocknobbler were to wake sleeping members of the congregation, and keep children in order.

*A History of Stourbridge, Nigel Perry (Phillimore 2001)

PART TWO

Miss Schtroumpf

And in that town a dog was found
As many dogs there be -
Both mongrel, puppy, whelp and hound,
And curs of low degree.

Oliver Goldsmith – 'An Elegy on the Death of a Mad Dog'

Monday 27th September

Sometimes logic is like a wheelbarrow engine, not to be found.

I receive an early morning phone call about a Schnauzer with a phantom pregnancy! Whatever on earth can I say to this lady? (The owner, I mean.)

At lunchtime I cautioned a grumpy Worcester ambassador of filth, this time on one of my favoured spots, the panoramic hill, Fort Royal Park, which is gloriously blessed with ancient Worcester pear trees. He was a Mr Livvid McOops, himself looking as old as the fruit trees and with more ink tattooed on his arms than there is in an edition of *The Sporting Life*.

I had stopped him for allowing his Lurcher, a typical 'scrufts' dog, to dump *un crapaud pilé* - a squashed toad - as Mammo, Magie's grandmother, used to say, albeit in a different context. Mr McOops was a mobile *Law Society Gazette*, a dabster who squeaked out hostility against authority. His final comment as I walked away was, 'We saw off Hitler, and we'll see off little Hitlers like you!'

I rested here for a while. The bench I was seated on displayed two inscriptions illustrating the best and worst of Worcester:

1) 'To Gerald Curtler 1909-1976, protector of animals.'
2) 'Lacey is a sad fat bitch ... Lacey is a hore ... Lacey is a shoe.'

The Story of Maria

I received a phone call from a professional gentleman in a posh part of Worcester. As always, it is a pleasure to respond to incidents in this sort of locality. Mr Hiram Bloorst was upset by some early morning barking which was fretting his night-owl daughter just down from university. He gave me in his own meek manner the description of every whimper, howl and yelp, in return eliciting from me the law's remedy concerning what magistrates would consider a public nuisance.

Then in self-accusatory mode, he said: 'If I had the nuts of a rat I would go around there and sort it out myself.' Nevertheless, I promised to make a visit to deal with it informally for him.

I arrived at the nearby Georgian residence in question, parking Pixie next to a Morgan, the most beautiful piece of metalwork in the world. This example, a Plus 8, was in gold livery and had Golden Rod written in black italics on the driver's door.

My ringing of the bell was met by a dog skidding joyously across a polished parquet floor in anticipation of the return of a loved one, before it went crashing 'crump!' into the other side of the door. This was then opened in an expansive flourish by the charming Mrs Maria Carissimi, who appeared immediately the sort of person who would understand other people's feelings. She was dressed in a casually sophisticated way resembling an older Natalie Wood from *West Side Story*. On initially scrutinising my uniform she welcomed me over the threshold in a typically affable American manner. She said, 'Come right in, what's your name?'

'Bernard Cartwright'

'You are very welcome Bernaarrrd.'

I followed Mrs Carissimi along a cavernous hall and into her kitchen, where a Kandinsky poster hung on the wall. A little girl and a young Red Setter attended. 'Look, Ah've had a bad day, would you like a cocktail?' said Mrs Carissimi.

I replied, 'I know all about bad days, but I'd like a cup of your coffee please.'

'Mah name is Maria Carissimi from Lackawanna, New York State. Are you from the police?'

'No I'm the City Dog Warden.'

'Gee, Bernaarrrd, that's swell and do you like your work?'

She started the coffee machine, so I had to speak up. 'Yes, very much thank you.' I then outlined my main duties – though today's work couldn't be bettered anywhere.

'So how can ah help you?'

'It's about your lovely dog here, does he bark early in the mornings? I mean loudly and outside? I have had a complaint about the noise.'

Her eyes reduced to chinks like a peregrine falcon about to

stoop; she said, 'Does he bark in the mornings? You mean The Council have come around here to talk to me about mah dawg!! He barks at 6am because Ah go to work at 6am; dogs bark. You English are so lazy, what's the matter with you all? Ah am in the service industry, employing well over 200 staff in my chain of hotels and Ah work harder than any of them; what gives with this "English disease", aren't you ever up for work?'

'Have you got all day? Basically of course, like much else it is rooted in vanity.'

She moved over to me and mildly caressed my shoulder; Her fingers didn't linger over long, but long enough for me to consider an answer: 'The "disease" as you call it, is something to do with the de-construction of civilization through audit mania. It is to do with the torpor which you rarely find in Switzerland for example but do here. It is to do with the frustration caused by the lack of democratic access to the products of the Royal Mint!'

'Well, mah dawg is just fiiine, look see for yourself. Anyway, who has made this complaint?' I was served with the drink and if it was not the finest Columbian Blue Mountain coffee it was very close to it. The ravishing Maria Carissimi, like most dog owners, in trying to alter my perception had steered the conversation away from those elements of her dog's behaviour which showed it as a public nuisance. In her case it was to the Setter's wellbeing and the problems of the 'English Patient.'

'It's not the dog, but the noise which is at issue here, madam. Can you please try and keep your dog in at 6 in the morning? And I am not at liberty at this stage to disclose the name of the complainant.'

'So Bernaarrrd, what happens if ah don't, or even can't do as you ask? Ah do know something about loud music because of my hotels.'

'We have a device, called a matron.'

'Am Ah actually hearing this, you have a what?'

'It is a tape recorder which can run for a week, and through using time code we can pinpoint the incidence and intensity of the barking. We then put the recording before the city magistrates, to consider it as a statutory nuisance, and ask for a noise abatement order.'

'Wow!'

Worcester Woman regarded my buff file which I had placed on her kitchen table, uttering, as if I was a McCarthyite communist weeder-outer, 'Do the Council actually keep a dossier on me!?'

'Not in that sense, no.'

I then played a little with her Red Setter and her child. The girl asked me, 'Why do puppy's bites not hurt?' I explained that in a litter each dog learns what pressure to playfully apply to the other puppies, but interjecting the girl whispered: 'It is because Pudding loves me so much.'

A child and her Pudding in love, so perfect!

The fabulous Mrs Carissimi then walked over and touched my shoulder once again, with the finesse of a brush-maker's bristle dresser. Her digits did not turn sensual. Many an old chimney can catch fire so a hardened sinner like myself has learned to discern motives in such situations as these.

'Look Bernie, tell the neighbours Ah'm only mortal, will you, please? So, Ah'll fix up a Bourbon party and just invite everybody around and we'll sort it out that way; they all share my bar here anyway, please just pass the message down the line and Ah'll be glad to meet your mystery person who doesn't want to talk to me about mah own dawg to mah face!'

'Sorting it out informally is always the best way, madam.'

I did pass this information on to Mr Bloorst, and Mrs Carissimi was as good as her word, and I never did go back.

Wednesday 29th September 1999

A day when I was eminently kissable and huggable.

The word pet comes from the French petit(e) meaning 'little one'. I would like to think that pets are put here to help us live in their world, where they have really very little to give except, of course, their love. Such a pet came my way today.

A Border Collie puppy was handed in to the police after it was found lost in the St John's district. She was absolutely innocent and adorable, having an unusual sheen to her coat, an animal straight from the whelp box, a 'shepherd's delight' surely destined for Cruft's. Despite the fact she was sick in the cage, she is the only dog I ever really wanted to take home. Like most of her sort, this creature brought to bear on me her doleful eyes, those engaging compensations for the mute state which dogs so easily use to hold sway over our emotions.

I subsequently received a call from a family in Comer Gardens correctly identifying their pet. Upon arriving to bring the puppy home, I was greeted by a string of children stretched across the road like the famous sequence from *The Sound of Music*. Before Pixie could come to a halt I was swamped by them and their parents, anxious to embrace both me and Rosco the Collie, so much so I couldn't get the van door open for the press of the crowd. I was just swept away by a community full of embraces. It was like the liberation of Paris. Today St John's rang out with mirth.

On my journey back through the centre of St John's I was following the traffic flow and travelling slowly as treacle in winter. In front of me was a old Ford Transit van and in front of that again was a Jaguar XJ6. The Jaguar saw the red light, but the Ford ran right up that great Jag's back. On impact the boot flew open and out fled a ginger cat, away down towards the Malvern Road.

The van driver got out first; he was noticeably covered with face fungus. From the Jaguar, three barrel-chested soldiers rose up, the tallest, a jock, in a full dress tartan uniform. One said to the van driver, 'You inconsiderate fool!'

Another asked, 'Where's Mrs Monty?' Then I had to move on, so missing the rest of this intriguing altercation.

Friday 8th October 1999

Up into Tolladine, a Council estate built upon a hill like a fortified Italian town and known locally as the 'State' of Tolladine. Like the old city states of Italy it has its own army, the Tolly Army, a rabble in arms which assembles, like packing dogs – or employers in a cocktail lounge, depending on your perspective – each Friday and Saturday night for the purpose of imbibing in the city centre. At closing time the older of the weary foot soldiers, wearing faces like Toby jugs and bellies akin to beer kegs, stagger up Tolladine hill following their dogs home. Just before knocking-off time, I happened to be in the back of the van when one of the local children, Janie Gipton, came to look in at the nets and the noose, perhaps hoping to see a dog on board, as I found children up in Tolly often did.

Janie's conversation with me went like this.

'My dog is not allowed out.'

'Oh, why?'

'I don't know. Can you tell me how puppies are made and what's the dog's part in it? We have a bitch I think.'

'Errr, ... well!' What was I doing talking to a nubile young girl about the facts of life in the back of Pixie? I wondered if I was being made a fool of, or just encountering the 'naïf' of puppy love, nevertheless I decided to exit as quickly as possible but as I prepared to go she ventured:

'My uncle had a dog once, he couldn't keep it 'cos the injections were too much, so he threw it in the
river! What's VD?'

Tuesday 12th October 1999

I saw another young woman whom I quickly put in my Worcester Woman book, named Victoria Quintus. She was seated by Severnside just along from the ice cream kiosk by the railway bridge, playing the cello to herself. She was not a particular beauty but she became one through performing.

I listened, to hear if she had Elgar's 'Cello Concerto' in her repertoire, but she didn't. Sometimes she peered at her brass music stand, and at other times just looked at the river. She played as if willing the notes to a lover on a departing vessel.

Thursday 14th October 1999

Mysterious anonymous leaflets appeared overnight pinned on the trees in the Countryside Park where I do a lot of patrolling.

Together with colleagues Peter and Derek, the Wood Wardens, I had previously taken some early morning action to hand out leaflets in the woods to try and stop the fouling of the Nunnery Wood section; this comprises oak trees planted during the First World War to replace those cut down for the war effort.

This was a reply:

So dogs on a lead must be
Not permitted to wander like you and me.
It must be all the cans they drop
All over the woods, outside the shop.
Dogs carve in our wooden seats misspelled obscenities
And drop their wrappers from their sweets.
Foul up the wood with all their screams
Disturb nature, imagination, dreams.
Dog owners mostly pick up the mess:
So they can read! Should parents do less?
Try training their children in manners and such.
Is this a hardship, or do we ask too much?

Friday 15th October 1999

'Defer to the Lord High Executioner!' – (*The Mikado*)

I received a frantic call from a Close adjacent to Perry Wood. Very few cities can boast of a rambling hilltop wood like this within their perimeters. It is the hill from which Cromwell bombarded Worcester.

Upon pulling into the Close I beheld every dog catcher's nightmare: a huge stud Rottweiler had fallen down one of the wood's retaining walls and all the gleaming negritude of the beast's form now faced me. I made one slow move towards it, offering peace in the form of dog food, which it just ignored. Because of the 'Grrrrrrrrr!', I could only get within a few feet of its appalling hulk, which contrasted with the white of its prize weapons. I was being careful to avoid eye contact, as a Rotty is angered by staring like no other breed I know.

For over twenty minutes I was stymied because kind words and food were to no avail. I could not get my lead over the growling threshold before its anger kicked in when I came close.

I thought of blowing up its nostrils to disorientate the animal by confusing its sense of smell, but didn't want to go face to face. Even the jingle-jangle of keys rattling, to give him anticipation of the thrill of going for a drive, was futile. I considered the net, but the problem was, how would I get a writhing and snarling Rottweiler out of a net and into the back of Pixie?

I telephoned for back-up but none could be made available. I asked for police support and was told, 'Let him go, and we'll pick him up later.' Reluctantly, I thought I might have to invoke the emergency procedures, which involved asking Sue to come out from the Kennels to use her sixth sense to entrap the dog. Failing that, if the animal cut up rough, the Council could ask the armed response unit at Hindlip Hall Police HQ to come and shoot it.

Most dog-catchers love dogs: many have their own at home, so the thought of 'disposing' of someone's pet isn't easy. This particular Rotty in one sense looked cute despite its gruesome face. When it tilted that head to growl, I noted that its ears did not go back, so I thought I would try one last act of doggie psychology.

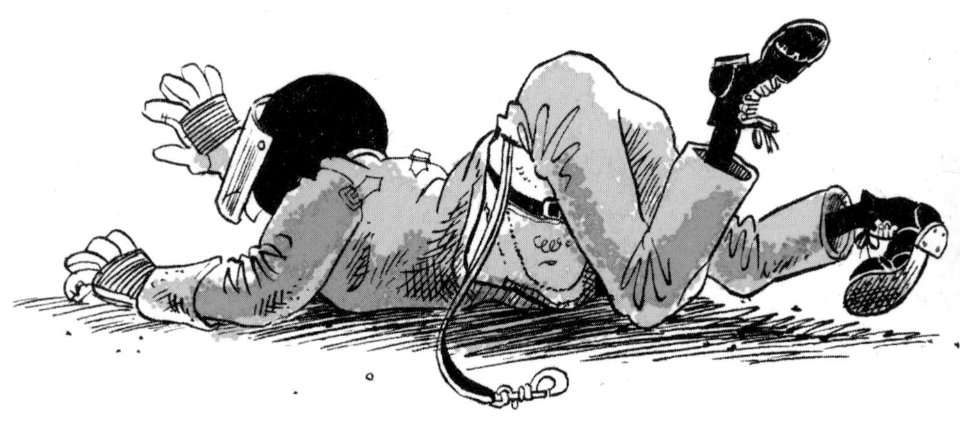

I put the dog food away, hid the lead in my pocket and prostrated myself before the dog like a priest before the altar during the Good Friday liturgy. Then by creeping forward on my stomach in an act of deference to the Rotty's authority, I broke the barrier. The dog was still seated in judgement above my jugular and, definitely not looking at his face, I put my hand into my right pocket, withdrew the lead and slowly and ever so gently clasped it on to his choker chain collar above, cooing meanwhile as though dealing with a dove rather than a beast which could have torn my throat out. Once he was on the lead I reversed on my belly, still in a posture of submission, stood up and then led him away to the van at a gentle trot with a 'c'mon' and a whistle.

The sweat broke out afterwards.

Over supper I told my family, who rightly thought it was hilarious.

The Story of Dirty Sixpence

Mr Charles Semele was a man who appeared safe in the assurance that both his seniority and his esteemed collection of pedigree cats would vouch for him every time he shot his mouth off in the smart Bevere district of North Worcester. He issued a frosty summons, with the request that I park Pixie out of sight of the portals of his house, to follow up his barking complaint.

In my limited experience, barking problems are mostly just extensions of existing neighbourhood disputes and this one turned out to be in that mould.

The complainant lived in a gentleman's residence named The Delph, surrounded by lime trees whose tops were on the golden turn. Two carved squirrels adorned its main gates. His front door was eventually swung open by a housekeeper who invited me in across half an acre of inlaid matting, for an audience with himself.

I entered the room to be met by a retired man in tweeds, looking seriously pregnant. He said, without any introductions, 'It's her blasted Collie, barking day in and day out, barking at you in the garden, even barking at the swallows. You can't reason with her, or the dog.'

'Hello Mr Semele, I'm the city Dog Catcher; when exactly does most barking occur?'

'All hours that God sends. She has a house full of lodgers and attracts riffraff day and night; she's not a full box of chocolates either. We are both from established Bevere families but the old duffer won't see reason. We all call her "Dirty Sixpence" because as a girl she once performed a rudery for sixpence, but we won't go into that.'

I urged, 'Have you actually asked her to keep the dog quiet?'

'No, not like that, no, I was hoping you would; you will won't you?'

I replied, 'I can only take action if you allow your name and address to go forward. The Council can't possibly enforce on behalf of anonymous persons or property.' Mr Semele winced like a man unused to being baulked.

'I see you are a rigorist.'

'Legally I have to run property against property; you could try a solicitor's letter, or let me have a quiet word first.'

'Yes, if you can get the old bat to put a muzzle on it or something like that. She's not very good on her pins, mind, and so can't control a dog: a cat would suit her better.'

I then heard the dog bark myself. 'There you are, you see!' spluttered Mr Semele, just on the enthusiastic side of gloating. A minute later his letterbox rattled.

'Ah!' I said, 'I think what I just heard is legitimate barking.'

'WHAT! What's that you said? Either you give me a very big apology or I'll go round there and kill it myself.'

'Making death threats against pets is an offence, sir. If a person approaches the front door a dog is allowed reasonable barking time and I deem what I just heard to be reasonable barking because of a delivery.'

'Gawd! She's a nutter I tell you, every bar fly in Worcester comes to her front door, she keeps an unruly house.'

Mr Semele was fuming himself puce with frustration, and my eyes were smarting with tears from the 'aroma' off his cats. I terminated the conversation with an offer to try conciliation with 'Dirty Sixpence.' My deliberate use of the sobriquet made him splutter out a laugh and brought his blood pressure down.

'I might offer her a barker-breaker, an electronic device which makes a high pitched noise dogs don't like, every time they bark.'

Satisfied with that, he ostentatiously bade his servant usher me out of the audience hall.

A minute later I faced a house as dreary as damp railway architecture with a wintry aspect. I started to walk up the lady's drive but hadn't crunched six footfalls of gravel when a cross-breed Collie came racing out to sniff a friendly odour from my hand and to look for an excuse to wag his feathery tail, display a ruff, finer than the one often depicted on Queen Elizabeth I, and to show off his fine bow moustache, unusual whiskers for a dog, though not for a cat.

'Who is it?' came a voice from the inside.

'City Dog Catcher, madam.'

'You had better come in, then, and take me as you see me.'

I entered a room of utter clutter, homely enough, but the only things in order were neat piles of the *Tatler* and the *Church Times*. Miss Sixpence was using a stare women deploy upon men as if gazing at a civic monument while at the same time taking in the chewing gum on the plinth.

She was the double of Queen Victoria, but with long Lurcher-grey hair, tied at the back in a way which reflected her age; in fact it looked as if it had been coiffured by loving wrens returning each spring to a storm-tossed nest. She was seated in a sun-faded armchair but looked better upholstered than it was, as the baggy seat failed to absorb her ample form. Miss Sixpence remained there and asked me to remove a crate of avocados from a stool and sit down.

As I did, I noticed that set at her feet were two mousetraps. She said, 'Oh, these stop the mice running up my legs when I doze off!' A side table was graced by a chess set and a decanter of sherry. In front of Miss Sixpence was a commemorative mug half filled with the brown liquid. It was 11 in the morning.

'Has my dear fat-gutted neighbour sent you around here? I guess he has, he's all stuff and nonsense. Did you see his cats? He's loaded to the gunnels with cats, he bloats them up with sausages for breakfast so they just loll about all over my garden making Bradley here mad, that's why he barks.'

'So he barks a lot then?' I ventured.

'I guess he does, but it gives the other neighbours a sense of security, especially at night. I grant you that if I have a tipple, what with my tablets and all, I may not wake up until 3 the

following afternoon, so sleep through most barking you see.'
With an effort she leant down to her pet and fondled him,
saying, 'You are mummy's good dog aren't you, Bradley?'

I was amused to note that her collie walked with the delicate
gait of a cat treading on newly dug ground - he was trying to
avoid the mousetraps.

Miss Sixpence employed her walking stick to point to the
sideboard: 'Would you like a sherry? The glasses are in there.' I took
out the only clean glass from about 20 available, all of them as small
as hospital dosing cups, and poured myself a drink. On top of the
sideboard was a stuffed pheasant in a glass case and on top of that

again a Bibendum, the rotund Michelin tyre man. Next to these objects a picture had been knocked sideways so I straightened it up and saw it was a photograph of a pre-war ERA (English Racing Automobiles) single-seater Grand Prix car with a slimmer version of my lady seated in it. Noticing my interest, she said:

'I used to share a drive with my brother, held a few course records in the historic class at Shelsley Walsh Hill Climb, the oldest race track in the world. I hung up my goggles in the early '70s when I began teaching abroad.'

As she took a swig of sherry from her mug, I asked her where she had taught.

'I did three stints in the old quarter of Beirut, mostly during the Lebanese civil war. I was a primary teacher of French and English to little ones. The kids used to nod off during lessons because they were up all night keeping watch in slit trenches. What a life! All they wanted to do was to go to Liverpool and see the Beatles, and to kill the enemy. One night two of my children were incinerated by a missile. We put what was left of them in an orange box and buried them properly the following day; their parent's wailing could be heard in Damascus – terribly cruel civil war.

'At weekends I sometimes got Mass in Aramaic which was in the Lord's tongue, it was a great honour. The sick people in the Lebanon were referred to as "The holy ones, the sick," and were anointed with oil from church lamps.'

Taking another swig, she continued, 'In the Lebanon we were being prepared for martyrdom; it was a bit different from Worcester! Mind you having said that, the British can be the most generous of people. You won't find a charity for blind budgerigars in the Lebanon, heh! heh! heh! So when I came home for good I did a bit of work for the St Dorcas doss house in the city centre, still keep in touch: but the legs, you see.'

After another gulp of sherry she said, 'Now look, about this business with Bradley, Mr Semele and I go back a long way and I know he is a widower, so as I go down to the family farm once a week anyway and as I know Bradley prefers it there, I guess I'll just leave him with the other dogs for the sake of keeping the peace.'

As I left Bevere I reflected that I had had a good result without applying any pressure. While Miss Sixpence may have been denied motherhood, she made up for it through motherliness.

Whatever she had done in the past to earn her nickname, it had been resolved through her service. She was no longer a Dirty Sixpence but a shiny sixpence and the Worcester Woman to beat. I was never again called to crunch her gravel.

Not a dog's best friend.

Worcester, like Bewdley and Stourport on Severn upstream, used to be an inland port. Today it was chilly enough for me to visit the lock-keeper to see if I could scrounge a cup of tea in Diglis basin. This is one of my more pleasant tasks, providing he doesn't tell me what has been washed down the Severn or dredged out from the bottom of the lock gates since my last visit.

During my saunter around the basin my phone rang with one of several dog queries such as I received each day.

Today's was from a Mr Cain Children in Pershore who expressed his feelings of the moment concerning the terrifying fate of his fawn Mongrel. While he was out his boys had walked their family dog as usual but allowed it to stray onto neighbouring property. Both they and the dog failed to see a ginger feline crouching on a window sill. When the mongrel was immediately beneath, the ginger beast descended onto its hapless face, sinking its claws into the stricken animal's eyes. The dog bolted, shrieking out its sufferings along the way, with the Tom on its back as if it were riding a race horse. At the edge of the property the cat decided to jump off but the howling dog just kept running and running and might be running still.

The owner wanted to know what redress in law was available to him for his loss? I gave Mr Children the same advice as I give to all such callers, viz, 'A dog has to be kept in order at all times.' Dog-against-dog incidents or dog-against-cat incidents or even dog-against-hippopotamus incidents are covered by property law, in the same way as if a neighbour's tree fell on your fence, where you can seek recompense for someone else's property damaging your own. Dogs are treated as chattels, so if an amicable settlement cannot be reached, any claim for loss or vet's bills have to go via a solicitor. But in this instance, as the dog was a trespasser it would be a question of what is deemed to be reasonable force and what disproportionate.

Had this cat been trained by cat-minders, validated by 'Ofform,' the Office of Feline Formation, under the New Labour proposals for pet welfare, diversion and amusements, this act of feline supremacism would not have happened. To digress, if the state has some shekels to give away for 'pet police', it should be given to the PDSA, the RSPCA, and for putting teeth into Dog Warden services.

It was two days later when I saw a dog answering this mongrel's description roaming down a railway cutting in Worcester, so I phoned up the owner for a more detailed description. However, until he addressed me as 'pecker head' I failed to realise that Mr Children was suffering from some sort of hitherto unknown neurological condition of the tongue, which enabled it to get around numerous other jibes, threats and blasphemies I'd never heard before, all because I couldn't return his dog to him.

Monday 18th October 1999 (Saint Luke's Day)

Thanks to kind Canon Colin Semper of Westminster Abbey, a former media contact, I once gave the St Luke's Day address from its pulpit on this commemoration day and was honoured to be part of the Abbey family. I was given the opportunity because I did a three-year contract as Director of the Churches' Council for Health and Healing, the ecumenical umbrella group for Christianity and medicine, based near Harley Street.

Initially, I used to relish my work, in particular leading lunch-time reflections on a text to fraught businessmen at St Mary Abchurch in the City, or helping to draft briefing papers for the Department of Health, like the one I did on depression. In the end C2H2 proved to be, for me, an unstable compound because of ecclesiastical politics and the baggage of Free

Masonry, all of which, at the time, combined to make the direction of the charity omni-credal rather than Christian. In its central direction C2H2 conformed to the cynic's definition of ecumenism as being 10 Anglicans 1 Free Churchman and a Roman, and I was the Roman. It was church unity built on sand and not on a rock, *in odium fidei,* as we say in the Black Country.

Lunch today in the Elgar Museum car park. Elgar regularly used to go back to Broadheath where he was born, almost to listen to it. Sometimes I have crossed the river and parked on the adjacent Broadheath Common, to get a sense of his presence and some peace, Elgar's presence being always greater than the

grip of my own fretfulness. Today I ate my sandwiches on the Birthplace Museum car park, as the Common, which is really a large meadow, was too damp. Here I regularly get away from the canines, to listen to the sanity of Nick Clark on 'The World at One,' imbibing as I do the sweet air of Worcestershire.

I could imagine Elgar consulting the Common about something little known about today, which he could never obtain: marriage with the violinist Miss Helen Weaver. Her father owned a shoe merchant's business opposite his father's music shop on the High Street near the Cathedral. She emigrated to New Zealand and out of his life for all time. Elgar's music is so very full of things 'beyond' … better places, dreamers of dreams, the unattainable and of departing souls.

On the Common I often sensed his music, just as he promised people would in this part of the world, with his prophetic 'Don't worry it's only me.'

Tuesday 19th October 1999

More 'rabbiting' than in Coneybury Wood.

People can often be typecast as either spiky or huggable, and this afternoon I spent a lazy few hours at ease with two huggable sisters who lived in The Arboretum. I had gone there ostensibly just to check their worry book of noise charts concerning a barking Terrier, which lived along the terrace and which, some of the other residents maintained, would be better off in a pie. Nevertheless, I stayed on to contemplate their bottomless teapot.

Discussion ensued about their recent overland pilgrimage to Santiago de Compostella in Spain. I remarked that David Lodge had just written a novel (*Therapy*) which featured just such a pilgrimage. I mentioned that I once visited his home in Northfield, Birmingham, sitting with his remarkable son and enjoying a glass of the amber nectar. I argued that Lodge's style was exceptionally lucid if unnecessarily vulgarian. These musings, on Council time, led us to consider the general proposition that too much explicitness in literature or film can rob you of your intimacy. This expression precipitated even more Earl Grey and skiving in the convivial atmosphere of the Arboretum literary appreciation society.

Thursday 11th November 1999

Armistice day in more ways than one.

No fun this afternoon. I was called to the home of a dying man by his two sweet Macmillan nurses. This was the worst case of dog noise I ever encountered. From a quarter of a mile away, with the window of Pixie wound down, I could hear the howling, baying and barking, so I didn't use my map for the last stretch but navigated on audio pilot alone.

I arrived to find a very sick man in his pyjamas propped up in his open doorway by the two nurses; through morphine and tenderness life still existed within his pinched features. I shouted out immediately that no one should have to put up with this row and I would sort this absent dog owner out pronto, adding that I did a stint as an ambulance driver at Mary Stevens hospice in Stourbridge, so was more than sympathetic to their predicament.

I discovered that yesterday a lady had moved in with the man next door and both had Alsatians. In order to make a phone call to the householder, who worked at the Police Headquarters at Hindlip Hall of all places, I physically had to leave the scene, such was the racket emanating from the two beasts.

Exceeding my limited powers for bringing such miscreants to book, I ordered Mr Peter Barkuss to come home and silence the dogs. He proffered an apology which I duly relayed. The nurses offered half a dozen kinds of thanks, though I could hardly hear them. The terrible effects of the noise nuisance now set to be addressed, the sick man crawled inside with the prospect of peace, to live a little, to shuffle some more and then to die.

Awful! Awful! Awful!

The Story of Natasha Fuhr, Part 1

I attended a Gypsy campsite at Coneybury Wood by the M5, the most scenic of motorways. I had had a report from a passing motorist about 'A Gyppo's dog attacking traffic' near the Cosworth engineering company roundabout. Because of this mode of expression, I suspected a racial motive.

I arrived at the encampment to find four drab caravans,

together with two colourful traditional wagons called 'vardos', and a couple of fine horses grazing over a ditch. Part of the site was made up of home comforts, with divans and crates to sit on around a smouldering fire, while the other end contained defunct metal products suffering from the injurious influence of rust.

I was scrutinising the dog in question, an otter-tailed Chocolate Labrador called Max which was lying next to a horse, when the dog came over to sniff my hand rather than to tear me to pieces. Then up popped a petite young woman perhaps seventeen years old, who in a Roedean school accent asked,

'Do you want to speak to my father? I'll fetch him for you.

She scurried away to find him. I had quite forgotten that Travellers' children, as well as learning the difference between a hip and a haw at their mother's knee, were perfect flag-wavers for private education. When she returned with her father and mother, Mr Fuhr equally politely said, 'Thank you, Natasha.'

Using the burred R's of South Worcestershire, Daniel Fuhr denied that his dog had been roaming. I told him, 'I would be loath to bring back a loved pet in a body bag, sir.' Mr Fuhr a wiry sort, warily friendly enough, went on to make assertions of his own about humanity in general. 'Do you know the root cause of the trouble in the world, think about it, it is the housed! Look at all the criminals, look at the mass murderers and the wicked, they all live in houses. Houses are the root cause of all the crime and ills of British society. Letterboxes and what comes though them don't help either. If people lived freely like us as Travellers, the country would be at peace with itself, wouldn't you agree?'

I did 'Think about it,' agreed, then left.

Early in the New Year I again bumped into Daniel and his wife Cora, together with Max their Labrador, at the Calor Gas depot at Shrub Hill. Leaning out from the cab of their scrap lorry, Cora shouted, 'We're by Powick church, come round sometime.'

New Millennium, new friends.

A week later I was driving on that part of the Worcester ring road called Wick Episcopi when Daniel's lorry flashed me, so I followed him back to their new camp.

Natasha had a rounder body than either of her parents but was dark enough to be considered a Romany. She wore Levis and her hair cascaded over a jacket top though there was no horseyness about her at all, in fact her state of being was reserve. Natasha had rather languorous eyes, the sort you could easily fall into. Her mother was taller, a Romany swarthy and elegant as any of Marc Chagal's paintings of circus performers.

Cora had asked Natasha to make some tea and when she returned, we chatted. As we did Cora opened a Kilner jar of pickles and I noticed how fine her hands were, so casually wondered if she had ever been in the circus.

'Why yes, I received my first sequins in a circus family when

I was six, travelling until I was twenty-six, when I married Daniel who was an erection engineer!'

Natasha shushed, 'Mommm! you're embarrassing us, you said we were not going to do that sort of thing to visitors anymore.'

'Sorry, I meant Daniel used to put up circus tents; you never did like smut did you my dear?'

'Certain things are meant to be private that's all. The circus is a medium which never turned blue.'

I observed, 'The circus is a medium which never aspired to the nonsense of delivering an audience to an advertiser.'

Natasha asked, 'Tell me, what does a dog catcher actually do?' So in outline I explained my main duties, but she concluded for me: 'We have a duty of care towards the animals. I mean look how they follow us about. Saint Francis once had a tame pet wolf called Gubbio. Animals must be attracted to the stillness in friars. Your namesake, Blessed Bernard of Corleone, used to run a sort of spiritual vets at his church in Sicily. He said the Lord's Prayer over the animals and afterwards led them around the friary cross, healing every single one of them.'

Daniel then observed with dry humour, 'Corleone! Corleone! Wasn't he The Godfather? Yes, Don Corleone.' He started to mimic Marlon Brando saying, 'I'll make you an offer you can't refuse!' which left Natasha stinging with humiliation. So, laughing his daughter's observations away, Daniel asked if I had 'ever tasted Gypsy Chicken Kiev.' I replied in the negative.

'Do you want to know the recipe? It starts with "first of all steal your chicken!" Ha ha ha!'

Natasha interjected 'Stoppit!'

Daniel said, 'By the piss of Johnny Foreigner, the cockroaches are taking over the larder here, can you get a muzzling order for daughters, Mr Cartwright?' He then passed me a tumbler full of mint Julep, which is home-made damson gin served over crushed mint leaves, 'Here, this keeps the cold out better than tea.'

To the swish of curtains the family then brought me inside their caravan, but there I was bowled over by Max who struggled up from his job as a peripatetic rug to rush indoors. 'This is our simple living carriage, it is a French adaptation of what we Romany people call a Bow Top Reading Wagon,' said Cora. I was bowled over metaphorically too, because the interior was

panelled in red mahogany and bevelled mirrors and the ceiling
was completely painted in the Venetian style in swirling human
figures and horses. In the bottom right hand corner I noticed a
faded motto but it was in old French 'Qui veult, peut' which I
roughly translated as 'Who wants can.'

'It was painted by a French artist about a century ago,' said
Natasha.

At the far end of the caravan were stacked rows of Kilner jars
filled with fruit, fungi and herbs, all neatly bound in white
canvas tape to stop them rattling as they went along and each
inscribed in black felt-tip pen. It would seem that Cora was, as
Ruskin once said, a person like 'The Queen of Sheba...with the

knowledge of all herbs and fruits and balms and spices and all that is healing and sweet in the groves.' Cora was the mistress of all things with which Worcestershire is replete.

Tuesday 16th November 1999

Called to Deansway Police Station to collect a stray; lingered awhile in the lock-up section of the Nick while the magistrates were sitting. A teenager, Asif Shampuddin, was on his way through the holding cage ahead of going up before the bench; as he did he asked WPC Becky Giblin if she had a light for his fag. She stopped, gave the kid a light and some of that special gift, feminine reassurance and mothering, even at the mesh, which is just what the frightened boy needed before he went up the steps. Becky is definitely now among my top choices for the 'Worcester Woman' award.

Met my colleague, Mary Old, whilst patrolling the Countryside Park. Mary works out from The Butts Yard, which is the Council Cleansing Department Depot. Each day she drives her white pick-up truck laden with bags of dog excrement, which she collects from the city poo bins. In spite of removing truck loads of dog waste a week, she never reeks of it. Mary is integrated into my network of 'listening posts' in Worcester, a methodology from documentary film days, but, in this scenario, to glean information about the canine threat. There is never a filthy fouler, starving puppy, lost fledgling or even a noisy rookery that is not scanned by the sharpness of Mary's gaze.

Friday 19th November 1999

I was called to see a woman about a dog in the largest private housing development in Europe, the Warndon Villages. To my utter surprise it was my young, elegant 'Worcester Woman,' WPC Becky Giblin and her husband. The officer sheepishly invited me in and ever so slowly sat down on her sofa, bidding me to do the same with a gentle pat on the adjacent cushion.

Becky then confessed to me that, out of compassion, she had recently taken away a lost puppy from Deansway Police Station dog pound, and she wondered what she could do about it.

Humility, the lady of virtues, is always a great thing. I didn't want to do this good and kindly copper for dog theft, thereby propelling her into the police disciplinary procedures so early in her career. So, as there was no lost puppy of that type on my books and as my scanner indicated there was no micro-chip in the dog's neck, nor was there any ear tattoo, I used the 'Ways and Means Act' and returned immediately to the Police Station to 'doctor' the police paperwork instead, thereby letting Mrs Giblin keep her cherished puppy. I am too old for guilt over such things as this.

Today I also found an old Black Labrador which was blind with cataracts and shot through with rheumatism. It had been tied to a bus stop in Warndon and abandoned. The orphan's leather collar had an illegible name and address written in felt tip pen upon it. Pre-Christmas throw outs - out with old, in with the new. Owners who do this should be sent to Dartmoor. Microchipping and dog ID cards should be obligatory.

Tuesday 30th November 1999

To a Road Traffic Accident just over the top of Tolladine Hill. A dark, well proportioned brindle Staffordshire Terrier had died instantly from massive injuries to its midriff; its eyes were bulging from their sockets. This breed is very low and much like cats, which are difficult to see on the road, especially at night.

I discovered this Terrier was tagged and after identification put the remains into a body bag. I went first to the neighbour of the owner of the deceased dog, explaining I had bad news to break, so we both went round together to knock at the door. The lady appeared and so I said to her, as calmly as I could, 'It's not good news, madam.'

She peered right past me to Pixie, which is a marked van, and screamed, 'No! no! not my baby!' She ran down her drive and banged the side of the van, shrieking, 'Let me have him, where is he? Oh where is my baby? Let me have him!'

And so I did.

PART THREE

Monday 13th December 1999

Bitterly cold – the dawn had left the sky as grey as a ram's backside and the trees looking like Disney chandeliers. I had curled up alone in St George's, Sansome Place, a building which far from being empty space was filled with colour and stillness. I was alone and yet not. With trepidation I attempted to warm my hands over the votive candles on the brass stand in front of the statue of the Sacred Heart. I was just below the Elgar organ which literally played its part in making Roman Catholicism acceptable once again to the English palate.

According to Byron, 'Man is half dust, half deity' (*Manfred*, 1817). Today, even in this 'Soul place,' I know which half I fell into. So, home to warmth, leaving the waifs and strays of Worcester desolate and dreaming of their hearth rugs.

Wednesday 15th December 1999

I woke up early feeling about as fresh as a jar of pickles but, as I couldn't find my obituary in *The Times*, I decided I had better rouse myself from my torpor and go to work.

Still suffering from the *mañana* syndrome, I tried to recover by dozing through a quiet morning patrol of Perdiswell Municipal Golf Course. However, my inactivity was forestalled by a small white starving Terrier hobbling across the car park and attempting to feed from what I at first thought was a discarded sweet or lollipop wrapper lying on the ice. Through the December drear I saw it was in fact a frozen used condom!

I slowly crept up on the poor dog, which then stopped feeding, vomited up what looked like a small ball of hay or brown paper, then, street-wise, made off into the tall sedge and freezing mist to possible oblivion. How demeaning for this lost, emaciated animal to feed on such human detritus! This, surely, must be one of the most degrading images and experiences of all my wardenship.

Monday 20th December 1999

Worcestershire, county of love. Middle England itself. Mistletoe 'as merry as marriage bells' harvested in Tibberton village today. The County has some of the finest meadows and ancient mixed woodland in Europe: mistletoe growing mostly on certain fruit trees like apple or pear and on some oaks and lime too. Tenbury Wells, Worcestershire's mistletoe centre, is known as the 'kissing capital of England'.

Home to Stourbridge and the Black Country, from being a daily economic migrant to Worcester. My first term of office, and the millennium, is almost over. In the evening we saw our youngest daughter 'Boubou girl' Rose perform at the Hagley RC High School carol concert.

Thursday 23rd December 1999

Christmas Day lunch looms large.

This is the time of year of Pitchcroft's metamorphosis into Swan

Lake as autumn struggles to barter with winter. Today I received a report of a dog attacking a swan on the flooded racecourse. I got there in under five minutes, not stopping even to buy some garnish for the bird. The fracas had even reduced the need for plucking feathers, which were already strewn on the water next to an Alaskan Malamute which was holding a platter-size cob swan underwater by its neck. This deed would remove the disagreeable necessity of the *coup de grace* – perfect.

However, a brave groundsman ran out into the flood and, at the penultimate gasp of the swan, chased the Malamute away across several acres of water and out of Pitchcroft. I was vexed, as Christmas lunch woozily unruffled its feathers, united itself with its cygnet and set sail again with the constancy of purpose of an avian *Golden Hind* in pursuit of a canine Armada.

The Story of Polly Seven Legs

Roaming is a curious thing. Cats are habitual roamers who invariably find their way home. Dogs are more easily disoriented. For example, there is roaming from one side of the Severn to the other, pursuing a bitch, or a 'Juliet' as she is sometimes called. This ceaseless following of the nose is not even hindered by a momentary whiff from the sauce factory. Then there is the terrified roaming after being spooked by fireworks. But the worst case I know has to be roaming-at-a-loss after being abandoned in a dog basket on the side of the M5 Motorway. This last privation must be much like the experience of redundancy.

From culvert to copse, from lane to street, the straying dog goes sniffing for something familiar along the way. For some inexplicable reason, to the stray dog mind many doormats have the word *Welcome* written on them, which in reality proves not to be the case. This paradox is further compounded, when, in an aggressive manner, a human appears and gives our dog, that symbol of loyalty and service, the new name of 'Shoo!'

My last job before darkness was to respond to a call from Shrub Hill Railway Station to pick up a friendly Wire Haired Terrier called Dash belonging to Jim and Soozie Rushock, who lived in an unpretentious house near Shrub Hill. This white dog looked like Snowy from the Tintin cartoon books.

Upon returning the stray, which spiralled with delight when released from Pixie's cage, I was invited in for a cup of tea while Jim wrote out a cheque for the stray dog fine. He told me he was a soft tissues salesman and was away a lot, like his daughter who lived in London. Soozie said that she herself worked irregular hours as a care assistant, pointing out that really, 'Dash wasn't getting the attention he deserved.'

I noticed that stuck to their fridge by some gaffer tape was a dog-eared cutting from the *London Evening Standard* containing a picture of a ballerina.

'That's our Polly,' said Jim, 'She's a dancer; the photograph was taken when we won our tussle over the grant to send her to Dance School when we lived up in North Staffordshire.' I nodded in admiration, then left after the cuppa, advising the family to get the Terrier tagged.

Six weeks later I picked up Dash, from Lowesmoor this time, and even though he had no tag and no microchip I recognised him immediately. Again, out came Rushock's cheque book. This happened three times more over the coming spring and summer so in the end I felt I had to waive the fine.

I saw Polly at home on one occasion; she told me her parents tried to 'wire up the hedges' but they couldn't keep the dog in the garden, as it nearly always dug itself out.

'We used to live on a farm near Stone, so Dash had the run of the place,' explained Polly.

I mentioned to her that if the dog was microchipped or had an ID disc, I'd return the stray free of charge as part of the Council service. 'I have taken nearly a hundred pounds from your mother and father and could have taken more, all for the sake of a collar tag costing £3.'

Polly assured me that she would press her parents to get one cut. As I left, as inquisitive as ever, I asked her which part of London she lived in.

'South of the river in Clapham.'

'Yes, I know it; I once lived in London for three years. Goodbye.'

It was late the following year when I was called to Shrub Hill Station again and there was Dash sitting on the platform edge. When I mentioned his name he came away with me easily enough. I walked around to the Rushock home and waited for one of them to return from work. They happened to come back together, and, as always, were relieved to see their pet once more. Without my saying anything, Jim said 'He was on the platform at the station, wasn't he?'

'Well, yes he was,' I replied.

Jim spoke slowly: 'He's waiting for Polly you see, to come off the Paddington train; we always went across to the station to pick her up but there is not so much of that now. Do come in Mr Cartwright; Soozie, I'm putting the kettle on.'

As we drank tea together in their tiny kitchen Jim said, between gulps and long pauses, 'Polly had a bit of trouble with the theatre, not the actual place you understand but a certain person. She had a crush on a man fifteen years her senior. He didn't see it in the same way.

'It went on for about a year I suppose, during which time

her performances were ravishing, she was dancing for him I guess: at least that's what she told a friend. The man in question was a Lighting Director. After the performances she used to ride her Honda over to his flat at the old match factory in Bow and just stand and look up at his window, nothing else. Obsessively compulsive behaviour, but who am I to denigrate how she felt?'

Jim lamented, 'She was at the top of her profession, she had perfect pitch and even if she wore ear protectors she could keep in time with the orchestra by feeling the vibrations of the music through her feet. If you marked the floor with chalk in rehearsal she always hit the same spot during the show.'

Soozie enlarged on this sad tale: 'Polly didn't have the swan-necked grace of a prima ballerina and she had short fast legs like that footballer chappie Michael Owen. Her nickname in the company was "Polly Seven Legs".

'It's all beauty and box office these days, isn't it? And accomplishment counts for nothing, and Polly's face really wasn't her most bankable asset. To be held back in her career was her second disappointment in life. Frustration can lead to anything, and it did.

'One night after the performance but before the punters had left, Polly threw herself out of a window and was only saved by a flag pole and some awning. She had fractured her pelvis, and oh the bruising! She'll never dance at that level again, poor fool!'

Jim concluded, 'Being a trained person, Polly was naturally resilient and so pulled through quickly. The dance company were very good about it all and pulled strings to get her assessed at the spinal injuries unit at Oswestry, as Os was more convenient for us than the hospital at Stoke Manderville, being as my patch is north of here.

'She has only just stopped walking with a stick and now barely refers to the incident. The fellow went on to work in broadcasting I think, and Polly has started in theatre administration in the West End and has met someone nice there. She doesn't come home that much as she also works in the theatre box office.

'All this is why, if we're not at home, Dash roams across to Shrub Hill Station, as devoted as ever, wandering round waiting for her to return.'

Friday 24th December 1999

Christmas Eve. Tiptoed out of the house so as to not wake anyone up. First time ever, no dogs or calls in the morning.

In the late afternoon, because of the cold, I found myself in the Cathedral curled up by the tomb of King John. Since the marble tomb was quite high and I was slumped behind it, my dark uniform making me camouflaged, I was unseen by a young couple who entered the dim chancel just as discretely as I had done, sitting on the opposite side of the King.

I guessed that they had come in, like me, to skive, rest or keep warm. It was completely dark but through the gloom it all started, imperceptibly at first, like an antennae tickle touch of toes in the marriage bed. I began to catch half-breathed yesses from these two doves, so much cooing, heat and suppressed passion of a county town variety, but enough for me to consider that the simile, 'as cold as marble', so fitting for the cathedral, was being usurped. It was a good old-fashioned snog and I had unwittingly assumed the state of the voyeur. As I adjusted my

posture, sliding even lower to try and hide myself, I discerned
that they were now renewing their marriage pledges of love on
the occasion of the millennium in this holy spot near the tomb
of King John, he who is buried for his soul's comfort between
two bishops.

I did try to slide away, but my Christmas presents in their
plastic bags started to make a crackling sound which I gently
suppressed. Through my rubbery garb I also switched off my
dog phone, rendering the people of Worcester open to canine
threat for the sake of not disturbing this innermost privacy. The
exchange between the couple is too intimate, too sacramental to
record – not everything has to be made explicit – but when it was
all over the Dog Catcher of Worcester just slipped away.

Monday 31st December 1999

Spent Millennium night sipping with a few old friends and dear
kind Father David McGough – now a bishop – at one of my soul
places, the parish rooms of Our Lady and All Saints Stourbridge,
this to the sound of fireworks exploding everywhere.

I live in the middle of Johnny Bull's own land where the
Black Country (BC) gives way palliatively to Worcestershire. Its
people were forged by the exactitude of engineering, the tension
of sinews and the self discipline of Non-Conformism.

The recent industrial deformation of the BC was Mrs
Thatcher's silent 'Guernica'. But there was no Picasso to paint
the pain and rubble here, like that achieved in his depiction of
the infamous Spanish Civil War bombing. Neither is there a
Dickens or a Zola or even a Lowry, to elevate BC dreariness to
the level of art, although Rob Perry, the local artist, and David
Lodge, writing in *Nice Work*, have made a fair fist of it. You have
to look to Paris to find art which shows the state feeding the
people, as depicted in the famous painting by Delacroix in the
Louvre, where Marianne, representing the French State,
symbolically bares her breast to feed the people during a tumult
at the barricades.

The English industrial 'reformation' of the 1980s caused
many here to suffer from VLAD, Voluntary Liquidation Affective
Disorder. The condition presents as Zombie-like behaviour
similar to that exhibited by those unfortunates in the West

Indies who were buried alive and then dug up again suffering from oxygen starvation. Many of the carers working with the afflicted in BC care homes, missions and therapy centres, are Filipino nurses, who before they are so much as trusted with replacing a loo roll have lessons in BC expressions. Here are some of them:

A nuss – a nurse.
The foad – the toilet or an out-house.
To do a dandelion – to piss in the bed.
A rodny – an idle person.
A reuter – a writer.
I ul – I will.
To blaht – to cry.
Off down the bumble hole – going for a walk.
A donny, a hond or a mauler – a hand.
Arse cream – ice cream.
Yed – head.
Ode – old.
A puss – a purse.
A wammel – a naughty dog.

There is a saying hereabouts in the BC that Satan himself once stood on Brierley Hill and declared that, 'Whoever came from here need never fear hell!' This on account of the furnaces and smoke stacks now long gone. The metal technologies originally forged in the BC put man on the moon, so not for nothing in 1990 did Saddam Hussain plot to build an atomic cannon here.

These descriptive sorties about my home always confront me as paradox, because one man's risk is another's exploitation and one man's 'Dark Satanic Mill' will always be another man's meal ticket. The attitude of the people of the BC, though, is something else, resolute and loyal as their Staffordshire Terriers but shy and dignified too and given to the silent smile.

To eventually know a BC person is like getting to know an observant Jew: it is to know them for life. In any crematorium, start a hymn or a prayer and they will finish it for you. They are the authentic 'Middle England' people, set in aspic and rather like the advert for their fine Banks's Beer, 'Unspoilt by progress.'

Friday 4th January 2000

It is the first week of the new millennium.

I had walked out at lunchtime from my Farrier House office and was crossing Crowngate Bus Station, when a bus driver approached me saying, 'Hullo, can I have a quiet word?'
'Yes of course; what's the problem?'
He ventured, 'Well, it's about this woman, or should I say her dog. On me outward route she gets on with her son who is usually carrying this Jack Russell, then she allows the dog to piss and mess on the bus; a bus is not a mobile public convenience. Can you do anything about it, because she's a surly cow?'
'Report her to your bosses and get them to stop it,' I suggested.
'No I can't, yer see, because I shouldn't let it happen in the first place and anyway all me mates would make a monkey out of me!'
Trying to be helpful I said, 'I can offer you a poo kit.'
'Is that all you can do?' he asks in a subdued way. 'Look, I have to clean it up with newspapers afterwards and swill it down with tea from me flask! You must be able to do summut!'
'I'm sorry sir, it's a private matter concerning a private bus company and has to be dealt with privately.'
The driver, Mr Pisswary Chenood, started to get irate, 'You mean if someone was murdered on the bus the police would say, "This is private murder so there is nothing we can do about it"? It's an offence - all I want you to do is catch'em at it; what do we pay our rates for?'
Before walking off I reiterated my position, adding 'You could put some pepper on the floor of the bus or perhaps some ammonia.'

Wednesday 26th January 2000

Monica Amblecote, a polite, nervous young lady, rang from Blackpole with a disturbing report somewhat rare in the annals of Worcester canine peccadilloes. A large black hairy dog would sit on the pavement all day for hours on end and do nothing except stare at her house. During the week I made several visits to the property and witnessed this phenomenon for myself. I was never able to catch the dog or follow it home, yet it always returned to sit motionless and gaze at this specific property, spooking the lady resident something terrible. There was no bitch in the locality for our suspected Romeo and apparently no previous occupier owned a dog. All I could do was routinely chase the dog away for her.

Dogs certainly have a sixth sense and I wondered if it was something to do with a death in the house but I didn't want to put that question to a nervous Miss Amblecote.

If a dog has an owner like, say, a farmer who works outdoors and happens to die outside, the dog, if it accompanied the owner at his death, may return to the very same spot to lie down and die itself when its time comes, as happened at a farm in Belbroughton, Worcestershire.

Emily Brontë's faithful Keeper, half bulldog, half mastiff (the people at the Brontë library agree with me that, in her painting of him, he does not look like a full mastiff), after he attended Emily's funeral, maintained a vigil outside the door of his dead mistress's room, whining every morning until he too died*.

Over the months my doggie visits to Blackpole became rarer and rarer and I never did get to the bottom of it ... creepy, but large black dogs are the ones which are ominously prevalent in ghost literature, such as the 'gytrash' in *Jane Eyre*. Dogs are always removed from a house during the rite of exorcism.

* *The Life of Charlotte Brontë* by Elizabeth Gaskell.

Thursday 27th January 2000

Not a cat's best friend.

I had to clear a street adjacent to a school when two Rottweilers ran amok, the madder of the two savagely killing a cat. I cleared the street to protect the public before getting the owner's wife to call them off. Thank goodness, a little boy, who witnessed the cat being turned into a rag doll, was safe - but it could have been him. All he would repeat afterwards through his shock was,

'Pussy dead! Pussy dead! Pussy dead!' I am foolishly not allowed to use firearms to protect the public in such circumstances. If I did have the right to shoot dogs, as is the situation in Spain, I believe I would incur the curses of the canine-loving community. However, this incident was one case where it was clearly necessary, and another example of requirements being made without the means to fulfil them.

Later on the nastier of the two dogs attacked a man, but I gather the police took the lead on this case. All I know is that the owner must have taken out a second mortgage to pay for the fortification of his house to keep the dogs in the garden.

After a month or two and following the second attack, during which time the owner of the Rottweiler had threatened to beat me up because I had passed my notes on to the police, I entered the Graveney House Council offices to pay in the weekly stray dog fines, and there he was facing me. He came over and in a crestfallen manner asked if I would now be a character reference for him and his dogs, since he had fortified his home.

Normally I would go half way with people, but my response this time was terse, 'I was there when your dog killed the cat and it could have so easily been the boy. Your dogs have regularly been out of control in nearby school playing fields, so sorry, chum!'

Monday 31st January 2000

A very, very weird and unexpected chance meeting today took me back again to the world of journalism and TV documentaries.

I had received a fouling complaint from a large property. Now, trespass is deemed to be a private nuisance rather than a matter for the civic authorities, who deal only with actionable offences in public places. On arrival I was invited into the sitting room to take further particulars, where I was given to believe, because of the people present, that I was in a type of government or security services 'safe house,' (not Salman Rushdie's). I discreetly took down the details and understood the specific problem posed by dog foulers loitering in the extensive grounds. I dealt speedily with the complaint, perhaps using more powers than I really had.

The following morning at 7.30am I waited for the fouler to turn up and then, as if I was on general patrol, threatened Mrs

Cornfield-Walker with prosecution for something called 'aggravated trespass in pursuance of unlawful intentions', under the Accessories and Abettors Act (Canine) 1861. Even if such a law as this existed, I couldn't possibly enforce it. However, it took effect, because the 'residents' from the property never contacted me again.

Friday 11th February 2000

Today found me watching Mr George Gordon and his pooch on the towpath in The Arboretum, where the accrual rate of filth is overpowering. The Arboretum is a densely populated inner city district, as far as Worcester can have an inner-city that is, and is not a wooded park as its name suggests, but it does have a pleasant canal meandering through it.

I had previously mentioned to Roy Fidoe, the Head of Environmental Services, that there was a deposit here every metre: thus we could get some PR value from this site. I suggested that we could put 30 flags by the canal, each indicating the presence of a mess, or get 30 tame members of the Kennel Club with their pets and then photograph them at this location. A full page picture in the Worcester *Daily Gargoyle* with the caption:

ARE YOU HERE?
WE WILL PROSECUTE.

would suffice. But nothing was ever done. Councillors do not want to upset the order of society, so dogs are not their principal focus, unless a child is attacked or they themselves tread in some muck.

Three councillors were particularly supportive of my work; there was the Worshipful Lady Mayoress, of course, and then the member for The Arboretum who once got me to dispose of a dead cat someone had left on his doorstep, and Gary Kibblewhite of the Bedwardine Ward who managed the golf range beyond Diglis and who had a nasty early morning fouler as a neighbour.

Anyway, I approached Mr Gordon just after his pooch, called Penry, excreted forth and both of them had slunk away with criminal intent. I looked in the long grass and saw a large stool with clockwise striations and stooped to do the finger test, to check that the deposit was warm and fresh, scattering a couple of enterprising flies in the process, but in truth I could have warmed my hands on it. I then cleaned my fingers with disinfected wipes. Meanwhile Mr Gordon had edged away with his animal. I caught up with him and asked about the noxious deposit.

He swore, 'By King Noll* I would never do such a thing!'

'By any chance, are you an actor from the Swan Theatre, sir?'

'There was never an English heath that was n'er fouled upon by an English foul!'

'The whole city is designated a no fouling zone, just pick it up please, sir.'

'Shit makes very good shoe polish, especially for tan brogues, tell the Council!'

'And if my aunt had tackle she would be my uncle. Just pick up the mess, sir.'

But when we walked back to the location we couldn't find the dollop anywhere in the grass, all we could see was something which looked like a slug in salt. He sighed and said that in future he would try and walk *behind* his dog so as to pick up the mess. We both chuckled with laughter and then he finally bantered, 'The earth closet is of great antiquity, tell the Aldermen!'

*Oliver Cromwell

Saturday 12th February 2000

Rose up early, did the washing up and slipped out to make my usual pre-St Valentine's Day pilgrimage to Stakenbridge Pool Meadows, Churchill, to collect snowdrops for Magie. Disturbed a vigilant heron, starker than the winter's sedge. I kept an eye open for the snowdrop warden because this particular expression of love necessitated an act of theft.

A great dog owner has died: Charles Schultz, creator of Snoopy. *The Times* obituary put it rather well ... 'Charles Schultz leaves a wife, two sons, three daughters and a little round-headed boy with an extraordinary pet dog.'

The Story of Simone

No account of local Women and their dogs would be complete without an appraisal of Simone. She is from a family of undertakers whose income has given her the leisure time to care for strays. Her remaining connection with Medlar's, the family business which she inherited with her brother, is that she still does the purchasing for them: coffins, embalming fluids and the like, and sometimes acts as a relief driver.

Her interest in dogs began some years ago, when she might turn up in a black van to take away the deceased from a house where a dog was left 'home alone'. Simone would take it upon herself to care for such a dog or cat until either the family claimed it or she could re-home it herself, usually through the breeder's association if it was pedigree. Her welfare work just grew from that, and now stretches out as far as Hereford. She would study the local press and, if she learned that someone had had an accident or ended up in hospital, she would make enquiries or even go round to the house herself.

But Simone first came to the attention of the people of Worcester as a 'ghostbuster.' The firm had a problem with a ghost in their Chapel of Rest. So, with all her clerical connections, Simone fixed up for prayers to be said for the deceased in the chapel itself and for a blessing of the building; yet the hauntings still continued.

Being an avid consumer of the novels of Anthony Burgess, especially *Earthly Powers*, where similar 'steps' are referred to, and being herself discreetly pious, she then arranged for it to be done all over again but in Latin this time, just in case the powers of the underworld cocked a snook at the bastard English language, but to no avail.

The problem was that the burglar alarm kept going off in the wee small hours of the night and, despite eight changes of parts and inspections to the electrics, it still tripped once or twice a week. It was assumed that ghosts could break a security beam. According to her younger brother, Horace 'Casket' Medlar, who looks as if he was established in 1912 like the family firm, Simone sorted it all out over one night.

Wearing a dark leather motorbike jacket for warmth and armed with a flask of coffee, a cross and a shotgun, making her look like Arnold Schwarzenegger in the 'Terminator,' movies, Simone decided to come to terms with this ghost. (Because of the wanton destruction of the farming community, by cheap imports of foreign food which make our livestock fetch no more than a beggar's ransom at market, illegal shotguns are easy to come by in Worcestershire – farmers can't afford the price of cartridges.)

Simone had secreted herself among the dead in the chapel, hiding under the staircase together with an aggressive Alsatian dog borrowed from a pub landlord in Tenbury Wells, when the ghost duly appeared and set off the alarm again. This particular apparition seemed, unusually, to drop down from heaven above rather than come up from the abode of the dammed, or even from purgatory's cleansing fire itself, for it was a petal from a wreath which had floated down off a high shelf and cut the security beam.

The undertaking business never really left Simone, so when dealing with the dogs she would often say, 'I will undertake to get this dog re-homed.' Or, 'I can't undertake that journey to the kennel until Saturday.' Or, 'I'll undertake to pay the expenses for that cat.'

The worst expression I ever heard her use was when her home was once the subject of a noise abatement order from Malvern Hills Council because of all the barking; she then said, 'I'll bury them!' meaning the complainants.

Simone's normal way of buzzing around the lanes of Worcestershire was to drive her Renault Clio with the rear seat folded down to accommodate a dog. On her hatchback a notice read:

CAUTION!
SLOW CORNERING
PETS IN TRANSIT

On one occasion, things were slightly different. She had to drive up to a farm to collect Foden, a very large St Bernard, and had requisitioned the firm's Daimler hearse to do it. The farmer, Jack Brazendale, had been taken into hospital at short notice and the community had rallied round to milk his cattle on a rota basis. Simone had come for the dog, but the spectacle of a hearse turning up at the farmhouse initially caused an awful lot of distress.

The registration number of the hearse MED 14R was made to read MEDLAR, a pleasantry which failed to add cheer to the occasion.

Simone had brought with her a rope which she attached to Foden's collar, knotting the other end into a ball, which she let flop outside the rear door. She then slammed the door over the rope, so that the dog inside was left standing on the coffin platform, yet restrained. This was all very fine, but every time she applied the brakes or Foden slipped on one of the numerous runners and slides on which the coffin went in and out, he jerked his head, making him surely the biggest 'nodding dog' ever seen in the rear of a vehicle, and providing a remarkable spectacle in the stop-start traffic across Worcester bridge.

Simone had more rings piercing her body than there are in a West Bromwich piston factory. This gentle form of mutilation distracting from her svelte figure, did nothing for her classical form. But her largest ring of all must be the unseen one she wears as a halo. On more than one occasion she has helped me out of a predicament.

A particular instance was during a nasty parvovirus outbreak, in which dogs can just keel over and die. Using her connections in the chemical trade she got me, free of charge, enough of the expensive special disinfectant to douse Pixie and kill off any possible virus.

Because of her trusting nature, every part of her had been mauled by dogs and I suspect if she were seen naked by the police doctor, out of context, her husband would be arrested for inflicting grievous bodily harm.

Her principal achievement is her extraordinary ability to re-home rescue dogs; she is Mother Simone of Worcester. Unlike some other animal welfare organisations, and even vets, she never once tried to off-load a dog onto me for support by the civic purse. Rather, she was keen to get dogs into the best possible homes and, like a social service adoption agency, would make home checks before even the placement of a cat.

Simone had a sixteenth-century cottage at Whoberley Chunter fitted-out like an eighteenth-century frigate. The flooring and doors are made from thousands of pounds worth of seasoned half-inch coffin oak, as found in decks designed for swabbing off. Her doors swing both ways and are customised to allow the full range with mop and bucket, enabling water to be swilled away underneath them.

Apart from a pet husband, Simone had nineteen dogs to care for and further progeny were always expected. The oak mantelpiece, which was as hard as steel, was a veritable garden of remembrance, for beside her pictures of Crufts a line of urns were permanently on display. The last ones in the line were inscribed 'Fudge', 'Lopez', 'Fuji' and 'Zazoo', the final urn being 'Captain Pembroke (Pem) Mayo Medlar RGJ'.

Each room of this 'bestiary', both upstairs and downstairs was dedicated to a particular type or size of dog, with the cats just living in the kitchen.

She was thinking about taking them all on holiday in a double-decker bus, accommodating people on one level with the animals on the other, like the illustrated children's book character, Farmer Jollybones, who once took his farm animals on holiday. Excessive zoolatry can be a defect, especially when other issues are pressing, but Simone managed somehow to avoid this pitfall. Never sniffy, always helpful: Simone, I miss you.

Thursday 18th February 2000

Assisted the police to break into a council flat in Warndon owned by a druggie, where a dog had been locked inside for the best part of a week. The Council drilled the locks out, then we put our noses inside to sniff for a corpse, but nothing was sensed. I had once spent a summer with the Coroner's Officers at Birmingham Central Mortuary filming all the city's unexplained deaths, so I knew the routine.

A copper went in first to see if a crime scene needed to be secured for forensic investigation; mercifully it didn't, so I was beckoned in to catch the dog, but I didn't need to because the Terrier had smelt my open tin of Pedigree Chum and embedded its face in it without my bidding, slicing the bridge of its nose on the can in the process.

The suffering dog then entered what I can only describe as a salivating fit, where it was too rigid even to eat and was only brought round by me blowing up its nose and dripping water down its gullet to cure dehydration and to make it cough, thus shocking its system out of spasm and back to normality.

Because of their genetic antecedents, or trouble at home, few drug addicts suffer from a single wounding. However, when you know you are likely to end up blotto on the pavement or even in hospital because of an overdose, dog ownership is feckless cruelty.

Sursum corda **('Lift up your hearts' – from the Latin Mass).**

As the Knocknobbler is a Church Dog Catcher, naturally I need to keep abreast of religious affairs. So Magie and I took a much needed weekend break, a million miles away from Dogville. It was an academic conference at Newman College, Birmingham, about Cardinal Newman himself, one of 'The Great Victorians' and it was characterised by a brilliant paper from Brother Philip (now Father Philip Cleevely), a member of the community of the Fathers of St Philip Neri, in Edgbaston, (The Oratorians).

Brother Philip quoted from one of my hero-philosophers, the late Elizabeth Anscombe, a noted Cambridge Professor, mother of seven and a cigar-smoker. The professor, whom I never personally met, was regarded as being as precise as a watchmaker's needle lathe and, possibly, the most accomplished reasoner since Aristotle. However, she was known to some of her students simply as 'Gem'.

Brother Philip recounted a particularly fascinating analogy which Professor Anscombe posed during one of her tutorials. This is the gist of it:

> Supposing a prisoner, who is serving a life sentence for a serious offence, receives an anonymous letter out of the blue stating that there is somebody on the outside who loves him and will send him in some goodies. The letter itself is not logical proof that the friend exists. The note sent in could be a prank by fellow prisoners or prison staff. If, in the fullness of time, the comforts arrive at the cell door and keep coming in and overwhelming the prisoner, their arrival is still not logical proof that there is a friend on the outside. However, the prisoner would vouch otherwise, saying that the presents are proof enough.

Christian faith may be considered in theoretical logic as lacking in evidence, but it answers the hopes of the human heart and seeks a response as a religion of invitation. Thus, to paraphrase Newman, faith can make its own evidence. Faith is therefore philosophically possible, as a mind can be taken over by a revelation. In a similar way true love is an act of faith because it can never be forced and only really be proved by mutual giving

and accepting. Only an open heart can be available to an open-hearted overture.

This was how Brother Philip, unknowingly, helped to elevate me from the creeping mental slurry of my dogdom. Our own saint, 'St Oomph', as our vet has been known to call Schtroumpf, in like manner, lifted my spirits when we got back home. With her eyes shining more than any bride's, ears sharper than any sentry's, she welcomed back those who love her.

Back to the dogs after the weekend conference …. An old lady reported a Dingo attack on a mourner in Norton churchyard. Must be the greatest case of roaming in the history of the world. Logged it in my 'phone and moan' book all the same.

Monday 23rd Februay 2000

A *cri de coeur* from a Health Worker, or it might have been a Social Worker, concerning a poor fellow who was coming to the end of his tether over a three-year battle with the barking from his neighbour's dogs.

Now the last time I had any sort of dealings with the Social Work profession, it was at a job fair in Brum where they were looking for trainees. There I was rejected by a white male Senior Social Worker on the stated grounds that I was 'White and middle class.' Not so today, because I was genuinely asked to help the client.

I visited Mr Martin Hussingtree, who answered the door to me in his underpants, and a face as long as Lowesmoor. His front room resembled the newspaper library at Colindale, North London; because copies of *Worcester Berrows Journal*, perhaps the oldest newspaper in the world, were stacked up everywhere like the Giant's Causeway. It seemed as if he had every edition back as far as 1690. There were, besides the papers, two piles of bank notes on his table each looking like the leaning tower of Pisa, one of £10 notes the other of fivers.

He fumed himself into a state, talking twenty to the dozen, so, as if from a mad dog, I backed off. I gave him some diary sheets to log the incidences of nuisance barking, promising this to be the first legal stage in noise abatement proceedings, but my offer in fact made him even worse, causing him to pull out the archives on his barking complaint all the way back to when Adam was in short trousers.

I really wanted to help this man like no one else I ever met in Worcester, even more so when he showed me the indentations on his wall from repeated battery with his walking stick. When he had calmed down to, 'Do you want milk and two sugars?' I learned that he was a former professional man who had come upon debilitating hard times and disfigurement through some sort of terrible accident or nasty affliction. I just wanted to put him in Pixie like a lost puppy and take him home. I promised I would try and get some sort of result for him.

The story of Natasha Fuhr, Part 2

Over the months I had learned that my Romany friends worked the scrap out of North Worcestershire and the Black Country and regularly crewed for a scrap boat which left Gloucester docks bound for Germany. Cora told me that Natasha had picked-up the radio operator's job on the ship: 'She speaks German like a native. The skipper calls her little Miss Marconi but we call her little Miss Macaroni to stop her getting puffed-up.

'We also have another nice little earner: we collect rare moss. Moss has wiped many an aristocratic backside over the years. We now collect it for the toothpaste industry, who use it to put the mint flavour in toothpaste.'

I learned, too, that the Fuhrs operated from several sites around Worcester and Hartlebury Common to accommodate Natasha's schooling. She had originally done 'trailer school,' a County Council provision for Romany children in winter but at the instigation of the then mayor of Worcester she was now doing 'A' levels.

Natasha had recently become a weekly boarder at the Leighton Dundas House School for girls at Frisby on the Chapel, studying 'A' Level German, Biology and English and on one visit to the campsite, I asked her how this had come about.

'A year ago one of my tutors put me forward for the West Mercia Juvenile Chamber of Commerce Award for Innovation and I won it outright, goodness knows how.

'Dad does the business of ridding farms of vermin; I go with him sometimes, so I did a presentation about a job out at Ombersley. We went to this farm at night and counted fifty rats around the chicken shed and barns. The farm cats and Max were overwhelmed. We caught a rat in a trap but kept it alive. I then went back to the lorry and got out a Calor Gas stove, a dixie can and a slab of tar. We melted the tar and dipped the rat in it ... . If Rentokil could have seen this! Oh my, the poor creature squealed terribly but we let it go again. The other rats refuse to live with such a grotesque colleague. They leave the farm and go away somewhere else, and all this for an outlay of under £9.

'I didn't say in my presentation that the rats went to live in someone's house a quarter of a mile down the lane. Like Dad I did the job for £50 cash in hand and half a dozen chickens. Payment can be such a ridiculous notion, don't you think?

'When I went for the prize-giving at Worcester Guildhall, I really made the businessmen laugh by saying that neither my father nor myself have ever entered into a transaction with the phrase "cross my palm with silver". However, at the end of my address they were rather more subdued because I summed up by saying that I had worked like a modern day Pied Piper of Hamelin, pointing out the famous commercial moral behind the story, one that the Pied Piper himself had mentioned, that social services needed to be paid for. It was afterwards that the mayor, Mr Hazi Hadarat, suggested to Mom and Dad that I do "A" levels.'

The following April, when the family were back at Coneybury Wood, they had a request to make to me. Daniel and Cora were going to work the scrap boat to Germany for three weeks or so and as Natasha was now away at school they wondered if, during my lunch hour on Wednesdays, I would take Max around there for her to make a fuss of him. The camp itself would be left in charge of old uncle Tad.

So I agreed, though obviously with the proviso that if I had any calls myself I wouldn't be able to make it. Well, it so happened that on my second visit I was late because of a dispute over a 'barking ticket', so couldn't collect Max from her uncle. When I arrived Natasha was already at the bottom of an ivy-clad bank which served as the perimeter to the school. She reverentially took Max out of Pixie's cage, then, making a fuss of him, served up a few of my dog biscuits and a drink of water from the plastic container. Natasha was late scrambling back up again and when she did she was accosted with what was really meant to be a jest from Mrs Barracliff her English teacher: 'You are a true Didicoy!'

I thought no more about it until the weekend, when I had to be in Worcester again, so called by the camp with a lost Cocker Spaniel puppy for Natasha to see. On arrival she handed me a copy of a letter written to Mrs Barracliff, but before I could read it she said, 'I used to go to Menith Wood Middle School when we were working the hop fields at Eardiston on Teme, and was regularly known as The Chav (the Worcester nickname for

Travellers). I was once cornered outside the boiler house by a gang of children who chanted:-

Chavvie Chavvie Wheeler!
Chavvie Chavvie Wheeler!
Führer, Führer, heil heil heil!

Her eyes moistened while I read the following:

Dear Mrs Barracliff

CONFIDENTIAL

Today you mildly rebuked me for being out of bounds. I have to say I do not know what bounds are, being an itinerant.

You also said that I was 'A true Didicoy' but you mentioned something else to me in the English class this week, something about John Milton and his blindness.

Blindness can take many forms. A Didicoy may not always be a true Romany though it is considered a Gypsy word. An Irish Tinker is not related to the true Romany people or little Egyptians as we were once called. We are from an ancient culture with roots in India and Egypt. By tradition many of us are performing artists, giving great pleasure to people in their stressful lives. We have contributed words to the English language like 'cosh' and 'posh', my favourites being 'pal' and the word used for pudding, 'gooi'. The persecution by Hitler, where 400,000 of my people perished, was one of many we have had to endure.

I am of royal descent from a Romany princess, of the lineage of the House of Gitanos. Long before feminism we had our lady chieftains. We are a highly moral people: few Romany people end up in jail.

Do you know how to catch a bird in a tree?

Do you know what happens during a badger's funeral by moonlight?

Can you make a pair of gloves for a doll using shrew fur?

Do you know how to lime a stream to provide enough trout protein during hard times?

Can you speak German or sing in Romany or Romansch?

I can do all these things. A rolling stone may gather no moss

I simply said, with as much heart as I could muster: 'Sometimes you have to learn to grow a thick skin.'

Natasha was to go on to academic distinction and I was never too far from that cheery Romany fireside.

That evening I pulled up very sharply in a tight lane in front of a moth-eaten whippet like a starving fox, just standing there alone in the middle of the road. Then up from behind a hedge surfaced a brawny man with a face like a Bulldog chewing a bee, and doing up the front of what appeared to be an old Montague Burton suit. This action tended to restrict his momentum, giving me time to assess the situation and lock myself in Pixie.

While he was making order of his attire, Mr Navelhazy started to shape up to me and then bellowed out like Ian Paisley trying to call time in a Dublin pub on St Patrick's day, 'You vile b****** I suppose you am on piece work for them w****** at Farrier House.' The scrawny whippet, alarmed by this original self expression, through shock more than literary appreciation, ran off. Now, a drunk with three fields of vision trying to get his coordinates on top of a ditch is as wobbly as a perjured chain of evidence. So when the critical mass of his bulk seemed to be over the point of his most unstable equilibrium I wound the window down and said, 'I am going to arrest you for being drunk in charge of a whippet.'

This threat to his intoxicated

ego, linked to his precarious posture, meant that, as a consequence of the laws of gravity, the City Council will not have to cut back that particular hedge for a year or six or seven! As he fell he uttered a 'term' which I have not heard before for that particular type of topiary.

Thursday March 25th 2000

There is little shame left in the world.

The Warndon Council Estate is usually high on my index of frustration. Today, though, some caring residents had found an abandoned starving Terrier and called me in. The dog was so caked in local red mud that she looked like one of those famous Chinese terracotta statues. Maggots were crawling out from her anus and her tail looked like a branch in winter so devoid of hair was it. Her legs were almost as thin as bread sticks when in happier times they should really have been more like baguettes. I initially thought it was a miniature breed but in reality it should have been a full-size dog, such were the ravages of starvation. Iniquitous! An appalling sight, for which the owner should be held to account.

As Pixie bounded along the road to the vet's I sang to my sad passenger, as I did to a lot of my dogs in order to try and cheer them up. She was dispatched from this life well enough, with me whispering 'Good dog' in her ear until the last.

One of the nasty long-running disputes in Worcester centres on two dogs which guard the commercial premises of Arson Crackles, the fire extinguisher firm. So I had to make a visit. As soon as I parked Pixie in the area, I was surrounded by local residents pulling their hair out, and rightly so, as the Dobermanns in question were astonishingly noisy.

Whether a case could be made in court was another matter because all the accusations against the owner fell away one by one when I suggested to the accusers that they put their names forward as witnesses for lengthy noise abatement proceedings, the standard form under the Environmental Protection Act 1990.

During my time in Worcester, the City Council, while fully supporting my work, were reluctant to take out injunctions against vexations to the peace of Her Majesty's subjects caused by nuisance dogs.

Eventually, two people were prepared to go forward publicly to denounce the 'Dobes' in court, but that was enough. Despite being warned about the threat of violence and the futility of the law in such a case, I went into the premises to attempt conciliation with the owner. What I found were two fine figures of men and if I had been opening a Worcester Man book, this would have been a promising start.

Mr Sulieman Gutt, the boss, came forward in a very friendly manner, as did his daughter Lullubhai, particularly when I identified myself as representing the City Council. His son Mynah Gutt, who had been standing in the doorway of a back office finally came forward too and introduced himself.

I explained that their Dobermanns had sight of passing traffic and were prone to bark at it, adding that I didn't see any attempt to restrain the dogs during the standard 15 minutes I was monitoring the incident. I suggested that they might like to bring their dogs indoors, as that was where their stock was kept. I further added that I was following up complaints from their immediate neighbours.

Mynah Gutt drew himself up to his full height and then held forth: 'This is all about racism! The neighbours this, the neighbours that, Pwaaa!'

Then something unnerving happened which I have never experienced before or since. His eye-line moved down from my eyes to my lips and his balance shifted forward as if in anticipation of some dramatic utterance from me like: 'You blacks,' or 'You Mosque boys', which he could later use against me.

When I proceeded to speak formally of the law's jurisdiction and the rights and responsibilities of all parties, his face actually fell. I believed I had been the victim of subtle racist mischief. Mynah Gutt then went on: 'This has nothing at all to do with the dogs.'

I sighed out, 'Then you have nothing to worry about sir, but the more evidence you give your neighbours the more ammunition they will have; please try and keep the dogs indoors,' I then left them on slightly better terms.

A year later, the matter sadly still rankled on, amounting to an awful lot of cat-and-mousism and unresolved barking.

Thursday 11th May 2000

At midday I paid a courtesy call to Mr Martin Hussingtree again, who stumbled to the door in the buff this time, unless he was wearing a particularly tight pair of long-johns. Speaking to him through the glass, I told him I was going to make a personal visit to Mrs Buskins next door to ask her to try and keep the dogs in order.

A minute later, my conversation with her was polite but firm, ending up with me telling her that she had to keep her dogs quiet or else I might return with an Environmental Health Officer to tape-record the barking for evidence, possibly for use in a magistrate's court.

Mrs Buskins leaned over and asked quietly: 'You do know, don't you, that he has a metal plate fixed in his skull which resonates and magnifies the barking?' I thought of the Council bill for specialist medical evidence in court, should she choose to contest the case. Made my exit.

I did, however, return to the location with Helen, a very thorough Environmental Health Officer, to put a 'Matron' in Mr Hussingtree's kitchen, but by then Mrs Buskins had made some efforts to reduce the barking nuisance.

The story of Gimzia

Gimzia is a lady I know a great deal about, though I hardly ever spoke to her. What I did discover was related to me by both a Geologist in the field and a Detached Youth Worker.

I first met her as a 'Thursday's child' when she went to 'The Social' for her giro cheque on Thursdays. I could always find the vagrants with their 'sympathy' dogs together sitting on the wall outside my office and I would issue them with poo kits. She had a Jack Russell called Rinty which had prominent, patchy, light-brown ears which looked as if they had been coloured in by a child in a playgroup. They always raised themselves in company like seated ice cream vendors on the arrival of a school bus. The

Terrier was also distinguished by a Union Jack scarf tied around its collar. Gimzia, who looked about twenty, wore an anorak, old Doc Marten boots, and a smile broad enough to go around the world.

I noticed that Rinty was tagged and made a positive comment about it. Sympathy dogs were always well cared for. I knew that Gimzia had a pitch by Foregate Street Station and would be seen there during rush hours. Between times she might be down by the Elgar statue to catch people going in and out of the Russell and Dorrell store. I had nodded to her there on several occasions.

The last time I saw her was when I had to search some 'void' property by City Walls Road to check for dog fouling. Gimzia told me, in jocular terms, not to worry about the mess because it was human muck and beyond my remit as a mere Dog Warden! So that was me put down.

During my first spring in Worcester, I received an intriguing call from a young Geologist called Emma to attend a disused factory site where she was working. We met outside, then clambered over the perimeter wall together, as the premises had been made secure. Emma's equipment was still in place; she was using an instrument at the end of a long cable to measure the methane levels at the bottom of the drains.

We went over to some old offices, which were locked, but the back door had been bashed in. She invited me to stand in the doorway and listen. I could hear nothing except the gushing of water from a broken tap. We persevered a few minutes longer and then there it was, a faint whimper. I whistled up the spiral staircase and the whimper became louder. Emma and I started to mount the stairs but on the way up she caught her cardigan on a nail; at her expletive the whimper became yapping. We entered the main upper office, which was like a cesspit, when Emma exclaimed, 'Would you look at this!'

Sticking out from a hole in the floorboards was the head of Rinty, as if she were in the pillory.

'How the hell did it get stuck in there?' said Emma, kneeling to caress the Terrier.

I said, 'I know this dog. and I guess she must have gone down a hole chasing something but couldn't get back up again. You stay here and I'll get a crowbar from the van.'

'There were some dossers about last week, so I backed off; I returned three days ago and the police and the ambulance were here taking people away; it looked like there had been a fight - maybe the dog belongs to one of them?'

'I think you are right, and the tag should read "Rinty" '.
While I was downstairs Emma tried the telephone number on the tag, but there was no reply.

It took me ten minutes to wrench up the ancient floorboards, and when I did we were again aghast, yet touched by what we saw, which looked like a living extract from a James Herriott book. Wallowing in ancient wood shavings and fresh excrement

were three Jack Russell puppies feeding off their mother's nipples, with the smallest attempting to suck from its mother's scarf. Rarely can the Union flag have been put to such a noble use.

Once released from her instrument of confinement, Rinty attacked a tin of Pedigree Chum which I had opened.

As we left, Emma decided, in addition to being a dog rescue service, to function as a canine herself: firstly as a sniffer dog searching out some scattered blister packs of pills, which were strewn all over the squat. Then to act as a truffle-hound cleaning up some disgusting half eaten jars of savoury delicacies and tins of pâté which must have made Rinty's nose twitch during her ordeal. By way of an explanation, Emma said 'I've seen skateboarders on this site, so we'd better get rid of all this.'

Emma wanted to foster both mother and offspring, so I signed them over to her keeping at her Bredon Hill farmhouse. Later I sent Emma a letter to thank her for all she did. Subsequent enquiries established that Gimzia had been badly beaten up and taken to hospital unconscious. When she was discharged, Gimzia used to visit the puppies at weekends, but I was often off duty so missed her.

It was a month or so after the puppies had left the whelping box and Rinty had been reunited with Gimzia that I put two and two together. I had noticed a certain piece of headed notepaper from the floor of the disused office, so after confirming my hunch with Emma I made an appointment to go and visit an organization which had the use of a temporary office in the old Ronkswood Hospital building.

Here I discovered Miriam, a Detached Youth Worker with the Sir Mordecai Nuft Foundation. Miriam was a streetwise thirty who dressed as a twenty-year-old fruity blonde. She normally worked out of an office in London on behalf of the Foundation. Over coffee she was quite open about Gimzia, especially when I told her about my involvement.

'She is safe, and is living in a hostel in Wolverhampton. She was at risk in Worcester because she was being "run" by a man who took her money known as "the Porch Monkey," on account of his habit of sitting in doorways all day long, that is, when he wasn't in the Irish pub.

'He is a reprobate called Adrian Bringsty, an ex-soldier. He wasn't really homeless at all but lodged at a farm off the Malvern Road and often came in by taxi to work the streets. We could never stop it because no one would give evidence. There had been an argument with Gimzia at the factory, and when a mobile security guard tried to intervene he assaulted them both, putting Gimzia in hospital. She was fragile, having an addiction to "tranx," so after the beating she went into convulsions. You know Gimzia never really wanted to work outside, begging and all that, because she would be alone with herself: this is why she had Rinty.'

'I saw the tranqillizers on the floor, along with with four tins of pâté.'

'The pâté was because her insides were raw through gin and drugs, so she had to eat soft food. I did initially manage to get her to see a dietician. Well, the guard at the site involved the police, so we were able to get them to pull Bringsty in. Gimzia has made a statement and some other street people have too, as Gimzia gave comfort all round.

'Bringsty is in Strangeways jail and will also be charged with six counts of robbery with violence in Manchester. During the fifth of them, he told the police, he took cash and jewellery worth £400 together with "Some silly foreign stuff" which he threw in a canal. The bags contained £10,000 worth of gold Kruger Rand! It took the police frogmen a fortnight to find it!

Anyway, Gimzia (her mother was from Corsica) has got a job training as a waitress on Intercity Trains, when she is strong enough to pass her medical, that is. She used to be a waitress during the Cheltenham Gold Cup races. The Foundation arranged the railway position and pays for her accommodation. When she is up and running we will put another person through the system. The only benefit of rail privatisation – contacts, you see! I will be working with kids around Bristol Temple Meads station next week before returning to the quiet life at Euston and Paddington, ha ha ha!'

'How does your set-up actually work?'

'The foundation is based in Hampstead, but I work the rail networks; a lot of suffering goes on at night around railway stations, so it's odd hours working for me!

'It all originally started after the Holocaust, when we set up a home for orphaned Jewish and Polish children. They were allowed to smash up anything they wanted, which was then lovingly replaced without any comment whatsoever. Everything was restored and made whole, all sorts of things were tolerated except violence. In this way we slowly got through to the children in order to make them whole again too.

'These days, people need counselling if they have a puncture on their bike!

'We have a second, more discreet service which targets unsavoury people in the cults and also in the pop music industry, those who exploit kids and even "roadies" for sexual gratification after gigs. I've been gawped at by many a "funkster," ha ha ha! Kids are screwed by a paradise of false kingdoms. Gimzia comes from Tetbury in Gloucestershire, do you know it?'

'Only through the silly tongue twister about two tired toads trotting to Tetbury!'

'Her mother went off with "Uncle Frank," Gimzia didn't want an "Uncle Frank", so she attempted to torch his antique shop: that's why she thinks she can't go back home. By the way, she says "thank you" for all your efforts on behalf of Rinty, she really appreciated it. If she settles in her new job I might try, perhaps next Christmas, to see if she would like to put her toe back into Tetbury once again. That's where the family estate is, near where Prince Charles lives.'

Three summers on, I happened to catch sight of a photo of Gimzia in a weekend magazine which was on the table in my doctor's surgery. She was seated in an open yellow Westfield Seight sports car which was covered in butterflies, attracted by the bright colour of the bodywork. The vehicle was parked outside an antique shop in Long Street in the centre of Tetbury and the blurb in the magazine referred to 'Gimzia Stern (24), a trainee community psychiatric nurse.' The caption read 'The Flower of Youth.'

Tuesday 23rd May 2000

There are a few things God doesn't know: how many dogs reside on the Dines Green estate being one of them.

I was greeted in Dines Green this morning with a report that a dog was seen running out of a sheep field with a leg of mutton in its mouth! I arrived at the location to a defensive greeting by Mr Tom Bogue, who went on to reassure me, as if he had been the paternal local squire.

'I 'oodn't worry too much 'bout it Guv, 'cos people am desperate around 'ere, no money see? They do their butchery at the slaughter site and must have sent a dog on ahead with a leg. We can't always trap coneys [rabbits], 'cos of the myxie yer know.' I had a peep at his attire to see if he himself was covered in blood spatter, but saw none.

The indices of deprivation rank Dines Green, Tolladine and parts of Warndon as some of the worst estates in England for multiple causes of impoverishment. People here are struggling through the militant thorns of circumstance, many on enduring state benefits, with the children having little to aspire to. A number of individuals seem to have an aunt called Mad Maud or a cousin in a secure unit. We are all genetic salads, struggling with the spiral chains of our own DNA.

Thursday 8th June 2000

The Story of a Male

The Evangelical Church on the corner of Cranham Drive hides a five-a-side football pitch which is used as a dog toilet for the Warndon Estate. I had run a campaign of signage in the area and now I intended to seek a prosecution, as the law was still being flagrantly flouted. I parked Pixie discreetly and focused my binoculars on a particularly dirty patch.

After an hour a man about six feet tall and casually dressed, a sort of fit walker type, appeared in my lenses. I got out of Pixie, clicking the door rather than slamming it closed, and shuffled towards him.

His old mongrel then stooped and fouled the grass, and the man moved off without picking up his mess. I followed him to the church, stopped him and identified myself, verbally and with my ID card, as the city Dog Warden. I asked him if he had any reasonable reason for not picking up the deposit.

He said, 'A dog has got to be allowed to shit!'

I answered that obvious comment by stating that this particular natural function was not a problem, but he had to pick the excrement up afterwards. I then invited him to do so.

He said firmly, 'No.' I formally cautioned him and asked for his name and address.

He wrangled, 'No, nothin' never, yer dirty c***!' and walked off up the passage towards the back of Sainsbury's.

I followed him at arm's length and said, on the hoof, 'You might as well tell me your name sir because I know you are local, so I will follow you home.'

He blurted, 'You will have a b***** long walk!'

After about a quarter of a mile he said, 'I am going to b***** hit you!' He would have needed long arms. For the next quarter of a mile he kept swearing at me, so I offered to go back with him to the deposit to pick up the mess but he again refused.

We then turned back on ourselves and he entered his house. I noted his number and then walked away to phone the office with a request to Kate to check his listing in the electoral register. As I was looking at my mobile 'phone I saw Rowland McAll, as I now knew him to be, exiting from his house without the dog but carrying a newspaper and walking with purpose towards me, his face flushed like a Worcester Pearmain. So then, I thought, he had had some sort of change of heart and was prepared to go half way with me.

I moved slowly towards Mr McAll and noticed with some glee that he was going to use a lurid tabloid to pick up the mess. Then as an addendum to the expletive 'You f******!,' he put in a right hook to the side of my head with his fist clenched inside the newspaper. Then one, two, he hit me in the face with his left fist, my glasses falling to the floor. The Knocknobbler had been knocknobbled!

Now I hadn't been in a fight since I was sixteen, but a Black Country Roman Catholic education circa 1962 did tend to equip one for such eventualities, something over and above the catechism lessons describing the 'fall of man,' a doctrine which history and now my own experience has vindicated, since Mr McAll seemed to have fallen further than most.

I had also had a certain 'set to' with Frank Bruno, the then British heavyweight boxing champion, when he decided, half in jest, to try and throw me down the stairs at Central Television, but I stood my ground and then, like today, it was my right fist aimed at my assailant's throat which changed his mind from trying further lunges.

Unfortunately, when I forced McAll off he saw my glasses on the ground and graunched them into the pavement with his heel. Had he come forward again he would have faced an improvised knuckle-duster made out of my car keys.

When I returned to the office, Martin Gillies, my line manager, noticed that my ear was bleeding so he photographed it for evidence in court. We returned to the site and photographed the dog muck and the context of the deposit. On getting back once again to the office, Roy Fidoe generously sent me to Sprosons, his opticians in Barbourne, to see what could be done about my specs.

The optician asked me how they came by such damage and when I told him he raved with delight because he ran a youth football team on the pitch in question and he personally thanked me for stopping it becoming a worse dog toilet than it already was.

The Council contacted the City Police and I made a statement to them. However, when they ran McAll through the police computer and realised he 'was in his 60s and had a clear 10-year record', they decided to drop the prosecution – a lame excuse!

The Council itself, however, did take up the case and Wendy, our solicitor, who once told me she knew of a child who had lost an eye through contact with dog faeces, ably prosecuted McAll, who was found guilty, fined for the fouling offence and ordered to pay for my new glasses, which he did by instalments. I forgave Rowland McAll, so when we left court I shook hands with him, as he had never once attempted to buckle the truth. Then he meekly uttered one of those ubiquitous Englishisms: 'It was just one of them things.'

After he had begun paying for my spectacles, I went around to his house and gave him the official Council 'Worthybag' poop scoops for picking up the mess. I did see him after that and he really did pick it up, if a little self consciously and with a pronounced wince; after all, he was a man!

Despite this amicable rounding off, how much abuse, biting and punching is a council official meant to take before an instantaneous and crushing reply goes over the bounds of legality? I spent some days reflecting on my outdoor work and semi-nomadic life style and its predicaments.

Monday 12th June 2000

I arrived at a house on a dreary estate following the invitation from an old lady, Mrs Beatrice Goggin. The back door opened onto her tiny kitchen and I was invited inside to be directly regaled with the plight of her Alsatian which was cringing and whimpering in the corner like a shirking living mat, but Mrs Goggin said, 'Oh, he's not the problem.'

She then shuffled her stooped frame across the kitchen floor, her slippers sounding like a fine sanding block slowly applied to balsa wood. She opened the side door for me to look out, and what I beheld was the appalling face of a Bull Mastiff, which was quartered in an outhouse and whose mournful expression would have made a funeral cortege turn up a cul-de-sac.

'It's 'im, 'e won't lay off me Alsatian.' Then pointing to the Mastiff, she reassured me, 'But Rommel won't attack you.'

How an old lady in a Council house could cope with two large dogs, one a fawn Mastiff the size of a lion, I know not. The problem was strictly hers to solve; however, a swift phone call meant I could get the huge beast re-

homed under the 'Ways and Means Act' without too much fuss.

An incident later in the day, if it is to be believed, used a device of the Devil and I had to think twice before writing it here but I do so now to illustrate the total destruction of mutual understanding and sacred kinship, not between people this time but between dog and man. Secondly, it illustrates that there is no revolting cruelty to which humanity will not sink.

I was patrolling the filthy path down to Diglis Weir and, just where the footway reaches the river, I fell in with a middle-aged man who sounded like Fowler's *English Usage*, but in reality he was a wicked, uncultured oaf. He had with him a large black Collie crossbreed. He told me what he had done:

'The dog bit my wife once in her own kitchen but I sorted the b***** out for it. I used to work on ships for the oil industry and have an old diving helmet. I fixed it up to the taps with some hose and then attached it to the dog's collar, while the b***** was chained up. I turned on the taps - you should have seen her in there - Ha ha ha! I could have taken bets on how long she would live. She nearly exhausted herself writhing about trying to shake the water out of the helmet to stop herself from drowning, especially when I turned the hot tap on full! Ho ho ho! Now I only have to show her the helmet and she goes and lies behind the settee.'

Well, I nearly kicked him. Frustratingly I have no powers of arrest over this violation. He doesn't deserve even one of my names except that of 'smell,' or better still 'sadist.'

PART FOUR

Doormat mightily upset

Wednesday 9th August 2000

Some days can begin like the action of a 'scavenger's daughter,' an Elizabethan instrument of torture, similar in principle to the device unscrupulous butchers use to crush pigs' heads for sausages. This morning was bright enough, as the dawn persuaded the August sun to come up and enjoy its cornflakes, but the day expired in anguish.

Now, 'barking tickets,' or informal warnings about noise nuisance, are usually easy to pop through letter boxes, but today I had sought to deliver one in the Bermuda Triangle of north Worcester: Blackpole, Cranham Drive and Windermere Drive.

Swaggering out from a yard by a line of dingy properties where human excrement is indistinguishable from dog muck to the untutored eye, came Mr Rampton Short-Fews. He was a stocky, nasty-looking man, as proud as a smoke stack with a crenellated top. He confronted me only 100 yards from where Rowland McAll recently attempted to punch my lights out.

He spoke up: 'It'll be cold in the morgue tonight, Josephine!'

I gulped and looked for his lobotomy scar.

He then exhorted me, 'Your sort can't see anything, can't yer read the bloody sign? There's nowt for yer here; if yer don't piss off, I'll give yer a knuckle sandwich.'

In fact there was no sign anywhere to be seen. Then, suggesting, to put it mildly, that I should go forth and fornicate, Mr Short-Fews postured like a territorially challenged Neapolitan pimp, shouting, 'Clear off or I'll hit yer so hard you'll come back with snow on yer boots!'

My right hand fingers moved ever so gently to fold over my biro in my uniform pocket. Now, apart from my family and my home, my biro is my most cherished possession and delight, because for me it is an instrument of life, vitality and ideas. Today, this prize possession had sadly been requisitioned for use as a stiletto, an unwitting means of possible mutilation or even death. However, I had the presence of mind to turn and walk away: this to the accompaniment of death threats. The incident very nearly deteriorated into serious physical 'knocknobbling.'

This precautionary fumble in my right-hand pocket had resulted from a futile conversation with the Council about personal protection issues and the law, when they denied me the possibility of having vigilant Schtroumpf with me for self protection. Nevertheless, I was resolved to defend myself in some way from the likes of Rampton Short-Fews.

I had considered a cattle prod-type stunner, but they are regarded as weapons ... quite! An anti-rape spray was another possibility. I even thought about carrying an improvised flame thrower using a water pistol filled with petrol with a condom dissolved in it, forming globulets of latex - a perfect use for a condom for a Roman Catholic! - In the other pocket a reliable Dunhill one-hand-operated cigarette lighter to ignite the petrol in order to replicate napalm.

Sometimes I did carry a little hammer to bash out dogs' teeth, should they ever latch on to me – bitches never let go! Steel-tipped boots were another option. I sometimes had a small screwdriver to perpetrate my own version of acupuncture in the event of an attack on me by man or beast. This tool is defensible in law and could be used either on the soft tissues or as a turn-a-key on a collar to apply a ligature to a dog's neck. Likewise, I had mastered a grip on Pixie's keys as an impromptu knuckle-duster.

Today though, it was my beloved biro which I was quite prepared to turn into a dagger. I was ready to shove it up the nostril of this man, or bury it into his eye socket and even, if necessary, push it through into the invincible ignorance of his brain, had his dark mind provoked his body to make the first move against me.

On re-reading the appalling intentionality of those above words, which were drafted earlier in the day, I realised I must quit my dog life. These expressions were to be the decisive facts which resolved me to get away somehow from this black dog farce, these terrifying predicaments and the emaciated dogs, such a despised encumbrance to their owners. The phrase 'my pet hate' seems to have a double meaning in such cases.

Monday 14th August 2000

The Diplomat's Story

My Church life never impinges on my dog work but, uncannily, today I almost thought it did. Now, I am loyal to all the teachings of the Roman Catholic Church because I accept the authority behind them, which arises from The Divine, the 'uncaused cause' who entered time to come and get us.

However, there is one area of ecclesiastical practice I disagree with and this drew me up sharply alongside the towpath verge of Worcester canal today.

The matter concerns the appointment of papal diplomats or Nuncios. I often wondered how these candidates are chosen. Today, though, I thought I had been appointed because I was addressed as a 'Nonce!', the French for Nuncio. Initially I thought this must surely be a meeting, arranged discreetly by the Vatican to convey to me the exciting news of my new situation in Rome, where I would be sent for briefing and training as a papal diplomat, indeed an answer to prayer! It didn't matter that it had to be done in the privacy of Worcester 'cut.' The job itself requires no sacerdotal functions of Holy Orders to fulfil it, so a layman or woman would be eligible.

In fact, in 1991, the Stourbridge Job Centre asked me to consider, would you believe it, if I would 'like to be put down as a Pope?' I had not realised that the Stourbridge Dole Office had as much influence as the Borgias, nor did I normally consider myself as papabile. In the end this offer proved to be a cruel misunderstanding and a terrible disappointment, because they really meant POPE, a Person Of Previous Expertise, a mere footnote to my listing on the Job Centre database, rather than the position of Supreme Pontiff, or supreme bridge builder if you like, within the Universal Church. This would have been a singularly portentous honour for a layman. Though the pay isn't much (Pope John Paul II left behind only a few personal effects), a nice house does go with the post.

But it was all a silly jape perpetrated in the Dole Office by well meaning people to thwart my pride, this capital sin always being problematic for me.

So, then, I was on patrol along the canal towpath in The

Arboretum district by its well known bridge, which is shaped like a storm drain, when I saw an old man and a woman leading an equally elderly Staffordshire Bull Terrier festooned in brasswork. They allowed the dog to foul in one of the dirtiest places in the city and one where there is a poo bin provided ... so much dogger excreting forth out of one tiny Wammel! They then walked away from it without picking it up, so I went to the deposit and took its temperature with my finger. I proceeded to stop the couple and invited them to return and pick up the said mess.

Mr Cleverley-McParker said, 'You're farting out yer ears mate, anyway how do you know it's my dog's shite?'

I responded, 'Because I saw you stand over your dog while it performed, then I went and took the temperature of the stool.'

Mrs Cleverley-McParker, whose name will not be on my Worcester Woman list but on my red list, then sought out an old supermarket bag from an adjacent hedge. As she showed some willingness, I offered her a Council Worthybag from my pocket, she took it and picked up the deposit.

As I happened to be working with my binoculars around my neck the man inspected them closely, he then looked me hard in the eye and pronounced, 'You are a Nonce!'

I replied 'Nobody has said such a nice thing to me for a long time sir!'

He blathered on, 'You are a pervert, I'm going to sort you out, you child molester.'

I was not being elevated out of excreta but plunged further into it.

'It'll be no good hiding away, you pervert!' quoth Cleverley-McParker. His wife then graciously gave me the 22nd letter of the alphabet lest I had forgotten it. He then ended with, 'We saw what you were doing in the hedge with that little boy yer Nonce! Nonce! Nonce! Get out of this yer Nonce!'

I released the pressure on my keys, which were lying alongside my biro in my uniform pocket. I took stock of this situation and saw myself doomed. If these two *crétins de première classe* made any hint of this serious allegation stick, the Council would have no option but to suspend me pending a formal enquiry. My reputation would be like dogger itself. It would be my one word against two of theirs. Can you imagine the Sunday gutter press? ... *'Worcester Dog Catcher Suspended*

After Towpath Child Buggery Fracas.'

I immediately phoned up Roy Fidoe and Martin and spelt out exactly what had happened: that two people were seeking to put my name forward for a child sodomy charge. My superiors were very supportive, indeed saying they appreciated my quick response and would deal with the matter in the appropriate manner and told me not to worry about it. In fact I knew that one of my senior and very helpful colleagues, Brian Kent, who worked in enforcement, had, in a previous job, been the victim of similar malice when he was falsely arrested on a completely fabricated suspicion of murder in similar circumstances.

The incident was another abrupt reminder of the vulnerability of Council staff. The police themselves would have had the Cleverley-McParkers in the back of a paddy wagon in two shakes of a puppy's tail. To my relief, nothing more was ever heard about the altercation: the two in question disappeared to manicure their pride.

(Over a year later I learned from a friend who was training for the privatised prison service, that 'nonce' is prison slang for a child molester who is segregated from other prisoners.)

I renewed my vow to grope somehow towards the exit door from Worcester's dog filth and threats.

Tuesday 15th August 2000

To work to write, to write to live.

Providentially, I met cheery old Mr Zorba Athalos again, who lifted my spirits, looking as he did like the Patriarch of all of the Mediterranean Islands. Despite his diligence on my behalf, the path by his home is as filthy as ever. We looked in silence at the putrefaction and then he spoke:

'Tellerme whya thee dorgs ere are nota fraid of you? Ina my country thee dorgs runaway when they see thee dorg catcher. Because, then "woumf" no more dorgs. Maker theem afraider of you with thee bullet and thee knife and you clean thee scum dorgs from Worcester.

'You Eenglish are all thee cricket and thee fine medicine.

Dorg ownas am thee beatnicks. You getta them outadebedlife by thee rings on thee noses and maker them cleena shit street 'ere!'

Katherine's story

At the specific request of Roy Fidoe I went on 'hot dog' inspection, patrolling the city centre open air car parks to see if any dogs had been left inside vehicles on this sweltering day. At the centre of Quay Street car park, which is located just above the head of Saint Cecilia on the Elgar £20 note, I found an estate car with a large mongrel inside, but the owner returned in the nick of time.

Later, I wandered down one of my favourite roads, the Tything, which has nearly twenty antique shops. Here I called for police assistance to break the window of a tiny Ford Ka in which a Boxer dog was flagging in the initial stages of suffocation, while the owner was perusing antiques. However, he too returned in time, irritated, though, to see me because of the prospect of having his car window bashed in, but a formal warning was sufficient to deal with the matter.

It was about mid afternoon, I guess, when I was stopped in the Tything by Mrs Katherine Bolshoi-St Vaast, a lady dripping with bijouterie and library books about gardening, so obviously from the County Set. Katherine was as refined as Roger & Gallet soap, except for her socks, which gave the impression they had been dyed in a Timbuktu water hole used by wild pigs for another purpose.

She lived out by the Lenches, where the police were once called when carol singers appeared on the doorsteps. As I looked at her, I thought how easy it is to get used to luxuriating in wealth. Katherine wanted to seek my advice about how to stop her Dobermann Pinscher attacking passing cyclists and motorbikes outside her country residence, where she didn't want to keep her gates shut all the time because of safety concerns over stationary traffic backing up down the lane. She also preferred her dog to patrol the grounds for security reasons.

Katherine hadn't got the first syllables of her request out before she had to draw up her willowy leg to her waist to steady the crumbling pile of books under her arm.

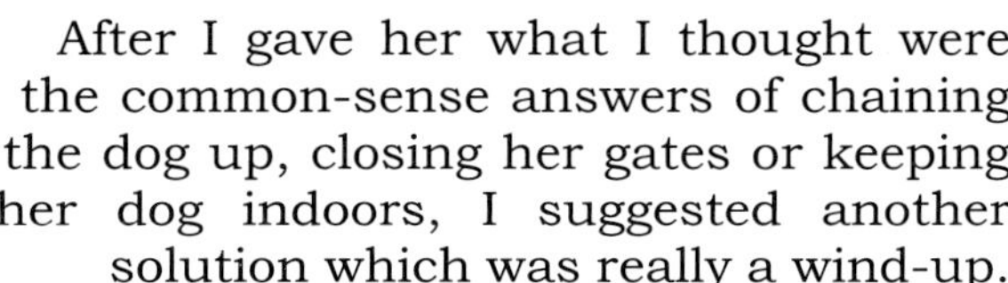

After I gave her what I thought were the common-sense answers of chaining the dog up, closing her gates or keeping her dog indoors, I suggested another solution which was really a wind-up.

I proposed that she got some help from a friend, one who had a bicycle, a crash helmet and a pair of stout protective wellingtons and an equally stout constitution to match. Then armed with only a rose sprayer full of neat whisky, I further suggested she induced the Dobermann to attack this stooge cyclist in order to give the aggressive dog a behaviour modification lesson by squirting whisky in its face.

'Mind you,' I concluded, 'The dog might get sozzled on the whisky and as long doggie legs and alcohol can prove to be a wobbly cocktail, yes, perhaps even keeping your dog permanently tight might be the most effective solution to your problem!'

What I said in jest brought melancholy to the face of Katherine as she replied: 'The situation we are in doesn't warrant the frivolity of what you are proposing.'

'Oh! I'm sorry.'

'You weren't to know, but last spring someone rode past our entrance, slowed their motorbike down and shot Jet, our other Dobermann, through the head, accelerating away to cover the noise of the shot. It was our gardener's twelve-year-old boy who witnessed the ghastly mess.'

'Oh dear, I'm sorry to hear it.'

'We didn't want any fuss or publicity, so we engaged a private detective who sat opposite the gates for a fortnight with a video camera and a fast car, but learned nothing. He did find out one thing though: the previous night someone in the village pub was boasting about how they had switched the throttle grip on their motorbike from the right hand side to the left of the handlebars so that they could wield a gun with their free hand. All lines of enquiry drew a blank and now we have only one Dobe, called Chigi; she was always the less frisky of the two.'

When I heard this, I cringed over what I had previously said, and I didn't care, or dare, to say that her 'problem' had in reality been partly solved by someone who didn't want a broken neck.

Re-ordering her tumbling books once again, with a sigh this time, Katherine said, 'Chigi is on a prescription diet now.' Then, lightening up a little, she asked, 'By the way, do you know where I can get discounted dog food from, somewhere like a cash and carry where it's wholesale? I'm not a member of the vat-and-tax club!'

'There's one up in Tipton, or Bilston way I think.' As we unconsciously drifted apart to go our separate ways she said:

'Oh, well then, thank you, you have been most helpful.' In reality I hadn't, but I had listened to her, which is what she wanted. Katherine walked away down the Tything and from the rear, with her gold and jewels hidden from view, she now had an understated elegance, which is perhaps as it should be, though I confess I was not looking at her socks when I made this observation.

Summer School

As I patrolled a play area in St John's re dog filth, Pixie was surrounded by eight little children and toddlers holidaying in the sun, all 'partners in grime' and curious about Pixie. Initially I gave out 'No Fouling' stickers galore. These were taken as presents to display to parents and siblings. When the assembly had settled and had finished searching Pixie for lost puppies, the children came around to me and the following dialogue took place:

'Why do you kill dogs?'

'I catch them to keep them from getting killed on the roads or from causing accidents. I really like to take dogs back to their own homes.'

'Why doesn't the Queen have a proper dog like my Dad's?'

'The Corgi is a proper dog, if a rare breed, and the Queen likes them.'

'My brother took his pants down and did a poo under that bush. Is that right?'

'No, he should really go to the toilet at home.'

'Why don't I get enough pocket money?'

(Cacophony).

'Why do dogs have big teeth?'

'Because they are meat eaters.'

'Why does dog poo have worms in it?'

'Dog poo is poisonous and can be dangerous, especially to the eyes.'

The conversation came to an end with a little boy saying, 'Ere, thanks for these stickers mister, can you come back tomorrow? because I like you.'

Monday 9th October 2000

Dog Wardens sometimes refer to dog theft as Dognapping. Today, burglars robbed a farmhouse while the farmer was out. Apart from looting all his valuables they took away the old farmer's old faithful collie He sobbed about it several times down the phone to me during the coming week, 'Why couldn't they let him see out his last days in peace? Oh why?' The dog was never seen again. This sort of sneaky theft amounts to moronic cruelty in my book.

Tuesday 10th October 2000

I backed off, not from an engagement with a menacing man or a howling, fouling dog this time, but from a former television colleague and his film crew whom I spied in my path, filming from the new Sabrina footbridge over the river. I didn't want them to see me in these circumstances. They had outdone me and were still in the industry and I knew they would laugh at my personal shaggy-dog story and really see me as a slob. I did not know how to respond to their expression of embarrassment on my behalf. For the first time I felt shame over what I had become, so much so that I had an ache in my stomach which could only be appeased by running in a panic and hiding myself.

So with my tail between my legs I blagged it into the nearby

County Cricket Ground on the pretext of looking for a stray dog. I took refuge in an empty stand, completely alone for maybe a hour or more, held there within the confines of my hurt.

Here I did what cricketers do when fielding boringly down on the boundary rope - reflect. I too was down on the ropes, fed up with working as a topographer of turds and dog spew. I was sitting on my own in not the most aesthetically pleasing cricket ground in the world, but, because of my depression, I felt I was sitting instead on the yellow firebrick of my own bespoke crematorium, which I had brought in here with me.

I miss documentary film-making because I miss the facility to move people deeply through film, that ribbon of dreams. Grief for my métier has never really gone away.

'My limbs are bow'd though not with toil but rusted with a vile repose.' ('The prisoner of Chillon' – Byron)

I yearn for my old job as, I guess, a celibate priest must yearn for fingers to caress his cheek.

I used to work in a documentary department, peopled with those of outstanding abilities, who wept with the tears of the world. Some scripted with their heart's blood, others, mainly Londoners, regarded Birmingham as the 'Khazi of the nation'. I was one of the few who worked both on network and on regional documentaries. Beer from Birmingham pubs and wine from Soho bistros went through my kidneys in equal measure.

In the mid 1980s I was invited to tea in the Athenaeum in Pall Mall. My host was well connected and I had come to trust him - ex military - Sir Nelson Pawsmorgue, whose nickname was Old Salvo. Over the ticking and tocking of the clock and the chattering of the newsprinter, which sounded like a magpie that had just received a tax bill, I was told in a stage whisper that a certain contact of mine, Comrade Ben Cough, was a highly placed KGB agent. This disclosure didn't bother me, though I was thankful for the consideration.

I was accredited to the Novosti Press Agency and had devised several programmes on Soviet dissidents.

The funniest encounter I had with someone who also had access to the highest grade of intelligence was with Baroness Caramba Pike-Otter. She would never shed enough light on the security services to attract a moth, and I knew I would be spading granite if I asked about it, but she did reveal something: it was not just by burglary or sophisticated tape recorders that we monitored Soviet agents but by 'Shoewatch!'

Our brave guys and gals would walk past known members of the KGB with eyes cast down looking to see how worn their shoes were or if they had been recently replaced. (This was the high noon of Thatcherism.) Thus the state had a cheap guide to the provisioning of Soviet agents.

The luxury of my maudlin respite in out-of-season New Road cricket ground now came to an end and so the Knocknobbler returned to work.

We all have bad days. Depression always throws me in on myself. It is like old people musing over what is now denied to them, which makes their present condition more bearable.

As I sauntered back across Worcester bridge I put my foot in a large piece of dog muck. I sniggered to myself as I cleaned off my shoe because usually if you tread in poo with the left foot it's good luck, and if it is the right, bad luck. I glanced at the west wing of the Cathedral saying to The Divine, 'Come, come, I am trying to get out of this!'

Friday 22nd October 2000

In the afternoon I visited a semi-blind man who lived near The Arboretum, Mr Edwyn Ralph. He is a good candidate for the 'Golden Bone Award' because on seeing only a moving blur weaving in and

out of the cars on Lansdowne Road, just by the school sports grounds where he lives, he rushed into the traffic to rescue this 'blur', which turned out to be a lost Terrier. He had previously invited me to his bungalow in June after I had picked up his dog's mess for him on the canal towpath. He had wept before me because he could not see his beloved companion dog properly. His sight had now deteriorated even more, it seemed to me, and when the lady owner of the rescued Terrier turned up to collect her pet, those vacant eyes were moist again at the dim sight of this happy reunion.

I had meant to put him forward to Roy Fidoe for a civic award, or publicity in a Council free sheet. However, one of the curses of humanity is that we forget, which meant that I didn't do it then but do so now ....

Requested to pick up a crushed dog by the Cosworth road island. When I arrived I found a large mangled cat instead. I left it there, albeit in a more prominent position to remind passing motorists of their own mortality.

Saturday 23rd October 2000

Doormat notified me of my failure to get an interview, for the second time around, for the Directorship of the cancer charity, the Hodgkins Disease Association, a post I was particularly qualified to be considered for, as I had had the disease myself. A scribbled addition on the rejection slip, possibly by an anarchic secretary, expressed sentiments genuinely wishing me well. I wonder if all my frustrations are really disposed for good, with rejection conspiring with time to save me from myself?

During the afternoon I travelled with my youngest daughter, Boubou girl Rose, and her friend Kate to Oxford for the day. Lunch with the Dons at one of my 'soul places', the Parsonage Hotel, off St Giles. Bummed around Blackwell's bookshop, buying them a book each, then ambled around the colleges, passing as I did the old dole office where, following my redundancy, I had gone looking for work, perhaps consultancy or possibly media work. It was here that I was offered a job as a 'Kissogram' gorilla!

The Bodleian Library was a must. On arrival we walked not into an exhibition of medieval texts but, to the delight of the two girls, straight onto the set of the first Harry Potter film!

Monday 30th October 2000

First call was a Council errand to the Jeep dealers near the Swan Theatre. In the showroom was a Hollywood-type set illustrating the rugged Rocky Mountains, which was a fitting backdrop for promoting the new Jeep. Unfortunately, the garage also displayed a life-size effigy of an aggressive grizzly bear. Sadly, the Jack Russell which was among the crowd in front of me didn't realise the bear was made of cardboard and proceeded to go into combat, causing the whole set to come tumbling down.

I came home to two rejection slips which had arrived simultaneously from different employers, one from the media and another from a charity. I might as well have been seeking the arse of the moon! Both concerns desperately wanted my advocacy when I worked in television and in fact I had put my career on the line for this particular charity. I am disappointed.

Thursday 30th November 2000

The story of the Battle of Worcester Poo

Unlike real battles, it all happened with surprisingly little notice: a Crown Court appeal against a successful dog fouling conviction to be heard at the Petty Sessions of the Advent Assizes of the Court of the Marches sitting in Ludlow.

I am sure my late Scottish mother, Catherine, sent a Scottish guardian angel to accompany me to court and look after me this day. He was in the form of Ron 'Rat,' the Worcester Rat Catcher who was work-shadowing me and who eventually became a Dog Warden/Rodent Operative for Wychavon Council. My amiable colleague, Ron Smith, was a former Scottish gamekeeper who had once loaded for Prince Charles, and he was a companionable man of the world.

As we travelled over to the appeal, and to make the journey

pass in a more congenial way, I began, as in the Canterbury Tales, to unfold for Ron 'The Fouler's Tale'.

This incident began many months ago in Henwick upon receipt of a complaint from a brawny builder who was threatening to use violence against the filth mongers on a public right of way near his home. I had staked the place out for several weeks but with no result until just after 5pm one afternoon when I saw a lady with her poodle. We were close enough for me to remember her if we ever met again. I lingered by a broken fence to see what she and her dog would do.

At about two cricket pitches distant, I saw her stand over her dog while it arched its back in characteristic fashion and defecated on the side of the path. I moved closer and saw Miss Orietta Loomiss walk away from the deposit without making any attempt to pick up the mess.

I scrutinised her actions with the greatest care to ensure she wasn't smearing the path with cocoa just to wind me up, as it was known in the locality that I wanted to keep the place clean. Swiftly, I went to the stool, and put my finger in it to see if it was still warm and fresh, which it was. I photographed the evidence, then moved on to apprehend Miss Loomiss. A few minutes later I asked her to stop. I identified myself and told her about the incident and invited her to return to it or give an explanation.

She said, 'How do you know it was me?'

'Because I saw you do it.' I gave her a caution and asked for her name and address.

Her response was to blurt, 'I'm telling you nuffin'!' She strode purposefully away into the gathering gloom. With no powers of arrest I had to let her go.

The following day I went to my local 'listening post,' a kennel club habitué, and, armed with a description of Orietta Loomiss and her white poodle, I received the intelligence I was looking for. My informant was precise to the nearest two or three houses, so I went around to the first one only to be met by a middle-aged lady who forcefully denied she knew this woman or her dog - strange, as she was standing ten feet from the front door of Miss Loomiss.

About a month or so went by before I saw the accused again, going into a local shop this time. She saw me but feigned she did not. I hid behind some fencing panels on the opposite side of the road. When she came out she was looking back over both shoulders but didn't see me.

I watched her return home and I then crossed a busy road and knocked loudly on her front door. There was no response but another neighbour came out; I identified myself as the city Dog Catcher seeking to speak to the occupier about her Poodle. The diligent neighbour replied, 'You want Orietta Loomiss, she is usually back from the works about now and yes, she has that sort of dog.' At last I had a name and an address.

The next day I conferred with my colleagues and we agreed to invite her in for a formal taped-recorded interview under caution. A letter was drafted which I duly delivered to her house. On arrival she was working on her car.

I said, 'Orietta Loomiss?' She replied 'Yer?' I placed the letter on her hand saying, 'It is about the dog incident, Miss Loomiss,' whereupon she took the letter and just threw it into the gutter.

She did not readily respond to the subsequent summons either, but her solicitor wrote in, calling into question my authority. When she did appear before the Magistrates, with one of the foremost advocates in the County, Ann Eyam, who earned her fees well, play was made with my dress through a claim that I was wearing a hat with a bobble on it. Mrs Eyam next produced a map and began to query the distances involved. Miss Loomiss took the stand and simply clocked my evidence out, through disputing my version of events.

The defendant was, however, fined several hundred pounds and stormed out of the court in an understandable sulk. I wondered if, at work, a plastic poo might eventually be waiting for her on a plate in the works canteen and she couldn't face the ribbing and the shame.

So to Ludlow for the Crown Court appeal; but it was as if I was the one on trial. I was up before Her Honour Judge McTiff and I was too nervous even to open a crisp packet. There were two lay Bench Members sitting with her, Mr Wilmslow Parsley and Mr Quock Lashim-Soon. The Judge presented herself as a buxom Pickwickian figure, a kindly woman who would not take the Brie off anyone's biscuit. We could not engage a certain campaigning barrister, by repute known to take no prisoners, someone Roy Fidoe wanted. Instead we had a silk of technical competence, Miss Orr-Pimms.

The hearing was set for the afternoon, so to lighten the day Ron and I visited a gun dealer during lunch. Ron was so considerate, as always. We discussed a problem here in Border country, where destitute farmers were shooting their Border Collie sheep dogs because they could not afford to keep them. Ron concurred that the practice was rife in Scotland and traditionally done by gamekeepers like him for a bottle of whisky.

The poodle-lover took the stand first and anxiously repeated the same invariant pattern of denial of most of what I said in the lower court, claiming ignorance of the particulars of the incident, even under cross examination.

In the early afternoon I took the oath to engage M'lady and M'learned friends. I was asked by defence counsel to display my uniform. So like a circus dog performing a trick, I drew out my navy blue rubbery fabric and pirouetted for the speculative gaze of 'the silk', emphasising the logo Dog Warden embroidered under my left breast pocket. The reason behind this thespian exercise, which was received with all due gravitas by the assembly, was to try and discredit my uniform as being far too unofficial-looking for upholding the law. It seemed as if I had taken the penitent's stool and not the stand. The great matter of my so-called hat with its long tassel, so important in the first trial, was not mentioned by the defence barrister.

While giving evidence I had an attack of heartburn and Judge McTiff sympathetically asked that I be given two glasses of water by the usher. So 'my' trial continued. 'Did I see the actual deposit from the distance I was away from the mess?'

'No, but the posture of the dog with the characteristic curvature of its crouched back indicated that it was making a deposit of faeces not urine.' I took care not to use the word 'shit' in this provincial backwater.

In answer to another question concerning the time of day (just after 5.00pm) when I had apprehended Miss Loomiss, the court considered getting an almanac to verify the sunset time. However, our solicitor wisely pointed out there were no leaves on the trees to block the light.

The defence silk, Mr Barkhat Wooff, using all the acrid politeness of the legal profession, dribbled an elegant discourse through my case, making much of the omission from my written statement of my finger test to ascertain the temperature of the deposit. I had mentioned it today because I had previously mentioned it in the Magistrates Court under cross examination by the defence counsel itself. It is, besides, standard form for traffic wardens to gauge the temperature of car radiators as an indication to how long a vehicle has been standing, the details of which do not necessarily get into their statements when they prosecute. Anyway I said I was 'not submitting the temperature of the deposit as forensic evidence.' (A DNA test from reference samples would have been compelling.)

The judge and the two magistrates retired to consider their decision. They returned with the solemn demeanour of Old Bailey judges hearing an appeal against a conviction for a capital offence. Judge McTiff had the decency at least to say that if this had been in another court, the verdict would have been different, however, she dismissed my indications of guilt, upheld the appeal and acquitted Miss Loomiss, in the belief that I did not see what I had stated I saw on that path.

While in this matter my finger had literally been in the shit, now I was plunged in it up to my neck.

In her summing-up, she did not admonish the appellant for previously trying to wriggle away from the legal process. In a further declaration, perfectly correctly, according to the Judge's legal lights, she awarded her £2000 costs from the public purse, as the defendant claimed she was stressed by the whole proceedings.

Thus the dog droppings in question were rendered an illusion and yet, if I was to be believed, possibly the most expensive turd in the history of British jurisprudence. The Knocknobbler was knocknobbled once again!

Of course, I had fallen under PACE, the Police and Criminal Evidence Act (1984) and its 'one against one' trap. This means that policemen or council officials cannot ultimately be believed on the basis of their statement alone, which is a ridiculous impediment for petty offences. Why make enforcement easy when you can make it hard? No one should be asked to enforce gormless laws. I shall not cry 'foul' again.

I retreated from the battle of Worcester Poo. As I did, I began to relate for Ron that in the late 1970s I was once successfully involved as the senior researcher in a TV documentary investigation which eventually evolved into a million-pound libel action, when ATV Network, *The Times* and the *Daily Mail* worked in concert on one of the biggest libel cases in British legal history - 'Orme v Associated Newspapers', or The Unification Church (The Moonies) against the *Daily Mail*. Ironically, this experience was far less traumatic for me than defending a statement about dogger on a remote Worcester footpath.

With Ron now gone home, I felt zonked out and as lonely as a village without a pub. So I took myself off to the Mug House in Claines, which must be one of the prettiest pubs in England, to quaff a couple of pints of Banks's Mild, in order to recover and write some of this down.

Two weeks later a vindicatory conversation took place between Roy Fidoe and a City Councillor who was, unknown to me, present in that Ludlow courtroom, in fact as one of the ushers. This councillor expressed great disappointment at the overturn of the original verdict and said we had conducted ourselves properly. It was mooted that we might appeal against the appeal to test whether the judge might have misdirected herself, but nothing ever came of it.

Wednesday 20th December 2000

Yesterday the mother of parliaments whipped away the legal protection from the human embryo, but today she strove to protect Reynard the Fox. Even the Natterjack Toad is now protected by law. Any bar from Wolverhampton to County Mayo could have put our leaders right on that one.

Friday December 22nd 2000

A morning patrol of the Countryside Park to see if Boots the Collie from Ronkswoood estate was worrying the badger set again, but he wasn't.

Already I thought I had seen Paul in Cathedral Close and on the second time, when I was certain, I introduced myself. He is Chris Tarrant's agent and operates out of Worcester. I had met them both during my ITV days. When I lost my job I had written to Paul asking if he could take me on as a client but he had replied that he wasn't in a position to, claiming he couldn't find enough work for his existing people. He was rather sheepish with me today as I stood before him in my uniform. I did not at all want to embarrass him so just melted away … . 'Who Wants to be a Millionaire' anyway!

In the evening I visited the Cathedral for the last time this year. Had the place to myself again, sitting in the dark to discover love of a different kind from last year's, when I was trapped in voyeurism. I was by the Great King's School Hall in the cloisters and it was the air of Elgar's gentlest piece, 'Salut d'Amour', which furnished that darkness and my own. Sublime end to the year.

3rd April 2001

The Slaughterman's Story

Today I was an apprentice slaughterman in foot-and-mouth ravaged Worcestershire.

I called at kennels in the morning to learn that Sue had been notified that their smallholding was within the feared three mile radius of an outbreak. The disease had now suppurated like a boil throughout the local area. These gentle people, Sue and Mike, were without words. There is a particular affective depression which attacks kind and sensitive people and they had it in full measure. I left the kennels with foreboding.

I returned there at 2pm to place a Heinz 57-variety dog which was looking for children and biscuits at Bishop Perowne's School. I was not returning, on this occasion, to A.E. Housman's 'Summertime on Bredon,' but to his wintertime.

While I was doing the paperwork for the stray, Sue received the dreaded call from the Ministry of Agriculture, or whatever their rebranded name is. The kennels were given ten minutes notice of intention to slaughter the herd of ten sheep and goats, all of them hand reared on the bottle as family pets – indeed they were extended family. Sue and her able assistant, Dave, ran into the meadow with a loaf of bread to lure their beloved pets into the enclosure.

A Japanese pick-up truck with a winch attached trundled

sullenly along the pitted track and stopped outside this enclosure, which is opposite the house. Two Ministry officials assessed their victims like Pierrepoint, the hangman, squinting through the cell door in order to weigh up the condemned for the practicalities of the rope and the drop. I was alone with the visitors at this stage, so had to go to the house to fetch a dejected Mike. Dave just walked away up the lane and Sue and Donna, a kennel maid, all of whom were friends not just colleagues, went into the kennel office.

I challenged myself: what was I doing here getting involved in other people's problems? Was it because I wanted to put a macabre and prurient spectacle in my journal or was it for the sake of Mike and Sue? Motives are often mixed: on this occasion I helped because it was clearly the very least I could do for my friends and their animals. Considering the appalling practicalities of the cull, the blunt reality was that the quicker it was over the better, for we all had to work very deep in mud.

The vet and his young assistant stood silent initially. The vet then produced a shiny steel pistol from the truck: it looked like a single shot derringer, the sort ladies carry in their handbags in Westerns, and so I had to stifle a nervous laugh. He primed it for firing, then we entered an enclosure which was as sodden as the Somme fields.

Without more ado the vet ran down one sheep by jumping on its back to slow it down. I opened the gate for him to manoeuvre the doomed creature to the rear of the truck, the assistant grabbed at the fleece to help steady the animal while the vet, still astride, shot the sheep through the back of the head and into the brain. It sank writhing and kicking in a pool of mud and blood; whether this was nervous twitching or not was hard for me to tell. Blood traced its way along a folded tongue which not all that long ago would have been sucking at a bottle.

I guess it was quick, but that is like a tricoteuse who holds the basket under the guillotine saying to the victim, 'It's only like a prick during shaving.'

This grizzly end was meted out to almost all the sheep, but then we were left with a clinging mother and daughter, their eyeballs rolling with fear. We went for the mother first and when we grasped her Mike shouted out to her daughter, 'Don't look at your mother!' Then bang, the report was muffled by the fleece

more than any of the other shots. The
daughter made a bolt for it past my left
side and towards the gate. I dragged
her down with a late rugby tackle on
to her fleece and brought her to the
vet. The distressed young lady fell on
her knees bleating in front of me as if
asking for mercy but the so-
called greater good came before
forbearance and compassion.

For my part, spattered in
blood and mud I felt like a
gauleiter assisting at a Gestapo
execution in a French village - It
gets easier after you have killed the
first one - I felt as if there was nothing left to feel.

Whilst the sheep were being winched on board the truck,
two-by-two as if into some monstrous ark, the goats were
brought forward next, easier to handle because their horns can
be grasped. I looked one goat in the eye as it was being held
between life and death, yet I glanced away, not that I should not
look upon that horror, but that God's guiltless creature should
not peer inside me, a representative of a 'superior species'. It did
not know that I do not support a derelict political philosophy of
making all things cheap, rather than supporting, in this
instance, the farmers, parsimony being the likely root cause of
this outbreak of foot-and-mouth disease.

Sue sauntered disconsolately up the track to survey the
squalid scene, her fist clenched not with suffering but around
banknotes, a tip for the vet and his assistant to assuage their
pain and their feelings.

'Was it quick?' Sue enquired of me, 'Yes, it was.' She then
said, 'We turned the radio up so we wouldn't hear the shooting!'

The kettle was put on.

Late that same afternoon and by way of a complete contrast, I
was accosted by a visitor from out-of-town Wyre Piddle, who
enquired of me the means to stop the snarling domination of his
household by an adolescent male Collie. He explained that trying
to talk to his dog was like attempting to 'explain jazz to a kipper.'

I indicated to Mr Stan Leveret that his dog sees him and his family as dogs to be dominated, not as people. 'You have to find the means of dominating him.' But if all else fails, including kindness and encouraging confidence in the dog, I let Stan know that these are:

TEN CANINE COMMANDMENTS

Rule one: No toast at the breakfast table or morsels at any other time.
Rule two: Any unprovoked growling, and the collie is put outside.
Rule three: One meal a day after the dog has clearly seen you eat your supper as the dominant male.
Rule four: Plenty of walks but at a time of your choosing, not the when the dog wants it, varying the locations from the ones he wants.
Rule five: When he pulls on the lead you just start to walk backwards and the dog will soon get tired of pulling.
Rule six: Move his sleeping basket to different places to assert your dominance over him.
Rule seven: Women tend to make dogs soft and undisciplined through giving them too much fuss and nibbles. Arrange for a transfer of all this affection and titbits to your own person, in full view of the dog.
Rule eight: Say goodbye to him when you go out, to show him you come and go without his hindrance.
Rule nine: Keep Classic FM on during the day to calm the dog's spirit.
Rule ten: Further naughty behaviour to be doused in a bucket of cold water.

Monday 1st May 2001

Nothing much written for several weeks. I have recently been rejected for both the post of chauffeur to the Mayor of Worcester and as a Rights of Way Officer for the County Council, whose own grounds I patrol. Feel so dispirited.

This afternoon, helped an embarrassed colleague who had just adopted a 'bear-face' dog. This is an Akita, a large ginger

Japanese breed sometimes used for police and military work.

Only a couple of days after the pet, named Sumo, had arrived at its new home, it went upstairs and jealously shredded up an apparent alternative centre of affection – the double-bed! I returned the dog to kennels for a week's jankers so that when it came back it was more appreciative of its new home.

Wednesday 3rd May 2001

Rather than give you my usual dog spiel, I want to share with you what happened to me today, within the shadow of Waterloo Station. In all the dizzy succession of nothings, which were my renewed attempts to get a decent job, none of them were ever like this one. I had an interview for the position of Charity Director, but the panel really could only perceive me as a Dog Catcher and a figure of fun, rather than as a former charity director who might offer some expertise. Trying to explain how I had come by my present métier was like trying to knot an egg. So I return to Worcester and its dogs.

Thursday 4th May 2001

The day ended with me in hospital nurturing a disrelish for all things canine. A shifty youth had handed a stray dog into Castle Street Police Station, but the counter staff saw that the dog was strangely devoted to the man and suspected that it might even have been his own dog which he was attempting to off-load.

I went out to the police pound to fetch the scruffy Border Collie crossbreed, a wily ball of mischief but one I am used to. Before even growling or, as I thought, raising its hackles, the Wammel exploded at me, lacerating my wrist before escaping. It is Reynard the Fox who bears the tag 'sly', not *canis familiaris*.

I had momentarily taken my eye off its hackles, those hairs by anger bristled. I had, too, ignored its tail, a communicative appendage of joy, which yet in stillness is more arresting than a policeman's raised palm. I had paid a high price for disregarding both.

I ran to the front desk with my wrist pumping blood. The staff, as always kind, put out a tannoy for first-aiders. Within ten seconds I was surrounded by police. The senior officer asked one of the Traffic Wardens, (in fact the noted blonde and kind Worcester Woman of mine, Rubrica Van Truck, who was also my city centre listening post), to stop the traffic outside the station and take me across to the old Worcester Royal Infirmary which is now an out-patients clinic. I had not been in this building since the pincers of that scavenging crab, cancer, put the bite into me during that hot summer of 1976 when I had Hodgkin's Disease, a nasty condition with a nasty treatment.

Rubrica, obliging and efficient as ever, asked the nurses to stop the blood which had by now soaked a couple of towels. The staff there were great with me, they arrested the bleeding and helped to get me up to Ronkswood casualty department. Ironically, the Wammel returned again to the pound looking for food so the police were able to trap it behind bars once more but it managed to escape a second time.

Subsequent enquiries at lodgings to the rear of Lowesmoor confirmed that the youth who had originally brought the animal in did have a dog answering that collie's description. A charge of wasting police time would have been hard for him to avoid but the matter was dropped.

Later I sent Rubrica and the front desk team a card and a box of chocolates.

I resolved to make that tyke's trying out all his teeth on me my last experience of this particular occupational hazard.

Friday June 16th 2001

Nothing much written during the spring and summer of 2001.

I did don my thinking cap once again when I applied to be Assistant Press Officer to Worcester City Police. Usually I don't refer to the police as 'De Babylon' as they do in Handsworth but I was close to doing so today. On arrival at the Nick I followed my own trail of blood stains across the Castle Street foyer carpet to where my counter staff colleagues wished me well.

The interview appeared to me to be straight out of the Institute of Personnel Management handbook and as a consultation was not particularly penetrating. I didn't want to appear dogmatic but I did make the distinction between the function of a Press Officer and that of a Public Relations Officer and I don't think they liked me for it. I thought it was prudent not to mention that I had worked with Roger Graef on 'Closing Ranks', the defining television programme about police stress, culture and corruption.

Before the interview was over I did a practical test on the phone where I was laughed at by a young police officer for wearing my headphones askew; this I used to do when I was a TV cameraman, enabling me to both listen to instructions and follow conversations going on around me. I guess, as age tends to curdle enthusiasm, I could have, unwittingly, communicated some of my reservations about the interview to him, so that, in the end I was left barking up the wrong tree again.

A few days after my doormat had been disturbed by junk mail from the Police Station, I saw one of the interview panel sauntering towards me down The Tything and I was minded to smash into this lady to ask what this was really all about. Had I done so, I would have given in to resentment and some part of what I believe would have died within me, so I abstained.

Tuesday 11th September 2001

The world is in shock.

Writer's block. I just wanted to put my arms around my dear children .... At tea time, we said grace and prayed for those who will not have any tea this night. Scrubbed out a joke I'd subsequently written about the internment of Afghan Hounds.

Friday 26th October 2001

Eco causes are not the first ones I gravitate to naturally when children are suffering in the world, but today I did. I found a decomposing dog among the flotsam and bilge of the canal at

Perdiswell. Rats were agitatedly consuming the entrails from the inside, giving the corpse unnervingly an appearance of life. Rather than attempting to retrieve this carrion for inspection and disposal, I used 'The Ways and Means Act' to further the eco-system by prodding the dog down to the bottom using an old branch.

Down the once loved pet went through the watery shades of death and disposal, like gratitude which descends to the dim and silty recesses of the mind. There, the animal was to be devoured not just by rats but by eels and perch too. I did not relate this story around the dinner table.

Later, I heard a confession from a vexed Mr Shufflebottom, who lives near Gheluvelt Park. He approached me about an incident which had been disturbing him for some months. Apparently, he was standing by his front door when his neighbour's Jack Russell was let out on cue for its evening dump.

As usual, the dog sniffed the nearest lamp post and then, dutifully heeding the advice from its owner, entered this fellow's garden for its evening squat once more.

Mr Shufflebottom continued: 'I kicked the dog, which ran as fast as it could go, back up the road and in through the open door and onto the settee. It snuggled up to its owner and ... died!

The owner came roaring out into the road, but I had slipped quietly indoors unseen. The word came down the street that the dog owner was prepared to kill the person responsible. I still feel terrible about it.'

'Look,' I said, 'This citizen was guilty of perpetrating a

private nuisance towards you by letting his dog deposit its dinner in your front garden. What possible good can come from your disclosure now? Mind, what you did was wrong, but let sleeping dogs lie .... ' We then both slowly started to have a fit of the giggles!

The day ended happily-sadly like the countenance of the finest renaissance angels beholding The Divine. Now, Spetchley is an area of fine domiciles with very long front gardens and in and out of these came a Jack Russell who was on self-walkies. The dog went into the ambulance depot opposite, (another place, I recalled, which had recently failed to be enthusiastic about my application for a job and had deposited junk mail on my doormat).

Anyway, back to the dog; I had tried everything I could to catch the pest, even inducing a young girl to try and put a lead on it, a risky policy if the Terrier were to turn and bite her. The nuisance was jay-walking in wide arcs amongst the traffic, when a middle-aged man appeared at my side, and a welcome apparition he was too, because he knew the dog, so we had it out of someone's garden and into Pixie in five shakes of a puppy's tail. Then quite spontaneously, my Good Samaritan said this:

'I was so glad to help you today: I like helping people you know. I am a Church of England vicar, though I am a Chaplain to the West Midlands Police in Birmingham. I am a liberal Anglican, so that I can be seen to treat people the same. It works for me, you know. A few days ago I had to minister to a situation where a police motorcyclist, "Mac" Walker, was killed; it was really, really harrowing.' His body shuddered in emotion at the recollection. 'He was deliberately rammed off his motorbike in the line of duty and he left a wife and four gorgeous children behind.'

I said that I once knew some of the Birmingham Police well and I was sure his ministry was worthwhile. The vicar thanked me for what I said and then shot off like a teenager with new trainers. I was glad he was a liberal Anglican and that he had found in me, a Catholic, someone comfortable to talk to just when he needed it.

New Year 2002

Let us have wine and women, mirth and laughter,
Sermons and soda water the day after.
Byron, *Don Juan*

To Normandy for the New Year to receive the healing balm of old friends Lily and Raymond at their home at Mont Aimé. We visited one of the great architectural sites in the world, the church of St Joan of Arc in Rouen. A little plaque on the wall suggested of St Joan that 'Fire had returned to fire through fire.' If, as the liberals say, she was schizophrenic, I still believe God can entwine himself around a psychiatric state.

Arrived back to Monmartre and Rue Lepic to be in the midst of the delightful company of Claire and Guy once more. Rue Lepic became famous as the location used for the joyful film *Amelie*, starring Audrey Tautou. One slight hiatus in the middle of our holiday, was when Lily asked me about a certain resident on a neighbouring farm, that she was worried about. It turned out to be the weirdest spectacle in French rural life, a Pit Bull Terrier with a retinue of about 30 farm cats.

Friday 1st February 2002

The story of Rebecca

One of the few privileges of being a dog catcher is having the time to stand and stare. There is freedom to wander down a lane to pick wild damsons in the hedgerows, or perhaps to lean on the parapet of Powick Old Bridge chatting to dog walkers and in the summer months watching trout taking mouthfuls of midges in

God's own hurrying aquarium, the river Teme. Today's perk took place whilst loitering in the foyer of a school which I had been asked to attend.

At the beginning of the third millennium, education can be seen as one of the enlivening forces of our times. My Uncle Harry, one of 13, was among the last people to be birched at the Stourbridge Union Workhouse, now Wordsley Hospital, such being the great liberality of the State. Whereas my daughter, Marguerite (Poupousse), went to the Sorbonne. From a Black Country birching table to the lecture theatres of the Sorbonne in Paris in three generations, such is pace of progress.

These recollections were prompted by gazing upon one of the hidden gems of Worcester, the statue of the martyr, Blessed Edward Oldcorne SJ, as I dawdled in the school named after him.

I was aroused from these day-dreamings by a teacher. He asked, 'Are you from the RSPCA? Have you come for the dog?' I replied 'no' to the first question and 'yes' to the second. I was then presented not only with a fine stray West Highland Terrier but also with the sweetest young woman attached to it by a flimsy piece of string improvising as a lead. This tail-wagger's good fortune was Rebecca's joy, and the dog's trust was their deliverance from the boredom of algebra and the novels of Jane Austen. For the Terrier, so happy with its new-found friend, had followed Rebecca Madresfield into school and she was mightily proud of her charge.

The master nipped into his office and returned with a digital camera. He then asked me to enter into posterity with Rebecca; I gladly obliged. As we posed with the dog, I whispered subversively, 'This is better than school.' Her simple reply of 'Yes' was as happy as could be.

Being so close, I noticed her face seemed to present the contours of a child who might have special educational needs. If in fact she was SEN, Rebecca was surely endowed with many other special gifts. I was glad that Blessed Edward's had taken her concerns about the Terrier seriously and had made a fuss of her but then this young lady was teaching us what human beings are really for, by illustrating through her actions that it is values which make us happy and not the restless requirements of the social and commercial fabric.

The Terrier went back to a good home and its finder, Rebecca, was the most sublime Worcester Woman I have yet met.

As part of the 'Surrounding the Stove' festivities to mark Chinese New Year, Magie and I were invited this evening by two dear old friends, Anne and Sue, one of whom had taken Chinese students as lodgers. While our hosts did try to enter into the spirit of the celebrations provided by the students, they were rather muted, as both had recently been abandoned by their spouses and their faces were still suffused with the pain of enduring.

One absent husband had even set up another family in a distant city, fathering two children in secret along the way. He did worthy work for prisoners of conscience. After he had confessed his adultery, he was told by his wife, 'Now you have made me a prisoner of your conscience.' If truth is the first casualty of war, communication is the first casualty of adultery. If people put as much energy into their marriages as into their assignations there would be very little divorce. Naturally, with passion all sorts of things are understandable but the question is whether they are right.

As the evening gathered pace and as the Chinese students, Ho-He and Yu Phat-Tu, became more animated and talkative, somehow the conversation turned to what I did for a living, which caused the young people visibly to shrink away from me, as they loathed dogs. I learned that in their part of China dogs are served on a plate and prepared for it in the same way as Europeans kill lobster. The meat is often tenderised by the secretion of adrenalin into the flesh through fear, as one dog is forced to watch another dog being butchered. This method was also one of the barbarities General Pinochet's henchmen used in torturing Chile's political prisoners!

Then it was my turn to cower.

PART FIVE

Beasts of England, beasts of Ireland,
Beasts of every land and clime,
Hearken to my joyful tidings
Of the golden future time.
George Orwell, *Animal Farm*

Monday 11th February 2002

Lucky as meeting a chimney sweep on my wedding day, for the people who interviewed me today actually seemed to listen to what I had to offer.

I had applied to be an Administrative Officer in the Child Support Agency located in Brierley Hill. This organisation is the one which pursues absent parents for child maintenance, or that is the ideal. For once the interview was rounded and genuinely professional. Even if I didn't get this position I believe that I had, at long last, been given a considered hearing. It was amusing to note that the Civil Service spoke about 'the appointment,' 'the position' and 'the post' rather than the job, the vacancy or the contract: no hint here of the Gadarene slope of impermanence.

Friday 22nd February 2002

Worcester Woman approached me with a 'Pensive sadness not by fiction led'. (Byron, *Tour of Greece and Albania*, 1809)

Up early enough to listen to the BBC World Service while on my way to look for a possible throw-out along the hard shoulder of the M5, but nothing seen. Later a shaggy dog was reported in Elm Green Close off the Bath Road, not too far from the motorway. I did a kerb crawl along the Close to examine the gardens and, while doing so, I exchanged waves with a typical Worcester Woman, in fact resembling TV presenter Carol Smillie. On my return trawl back down towards Bath Road I stopped while this lady, who had the cutest Black Labrador puppy, came over to Pixie. I got out to stroke this doughy bundle of sunlight, a creature so fresh from its mother.

The owner had a face which was crannied by time's insidious

presence, yet she appeared to have created a place in her heart
where no bad thing could really touch her. She buoyantly said:
'This is Angus; it is his first day out. I am a widow, my husband
died last autumn; do you think Angus will be perfect for me?'

'Yes, quite perfect Madam.'

She then added, almost in rhapsody, 'You know, they need
looking after, attention and care, with brushing every day. Oh!
oh he is perfect!'

'I hope you will have many happy days with your pet.'

Nothing much more was really spoken between us. I'd been
in muddy fields and on the Motorway embankment since before
dawn and she had found a new husband and wanted to show
him off – a warm encounter and an antidote to our respective
lots. It is one of the few times on the dogs when I wanted to shed
tears of hardcore.

> *And Angus said, in one year more*
> *If fruitless hope was pass'd away,*
> *His fondest scruples should be o'er,*
> *And he would name their nuptial day.*
> (Byron, *Hours of Idleness*, 1807)

Tuesday 5th March 2002

Up to Tolly to attend a hit-and-run accident where a Staffy had
been crushed under the wheel of a lorry which didn't bother to
stop. I found the dog cowering under the table of a kind family
who had taken the injured pet into their home on Maple Avenue.
Its legs were splayed out behind it and it was peeing blood. It
screamed when I picked it up. Not a bark, not a whine but a
scream I have never heard a dog make before. I took the Staffy
to Mr Walker's Surgery, and it arrived awash in its own vomit.

He diagnosed a crushed pelvis like the sort motorbikers get;
he pronounced one word, 'euthanasia': the very name sounds
like a beautiful flower rather than a term for direct killing. We
conferred with the Council, as the dog had no ID and then did
the deed. As we worked I just kept whispering into the dog's ear,
'Daddy's good dog, daddy's good dog,' until it limply ceased
hearing whispers. Mr Walker said, 'Once you have put a couple
of dogs down you easily get used to it. If euthanasia came about,

busy medics would find the same and be tempted to see it as an all too familiar procedure.'

Tuesday 12th March 2002

Yesss! My porch rang aloud with gaiety because at last doormat had had a serious letter from the Child Support Agency offering me a post. But it was 'paradise postponed' for the letter went on to state that, whilst I had been successful, they were not able to offer me a position just yet, due to 'circumstances.' I knew all about 'circumstances.'

Doormat was muted in its jubilation and it was left up to *The Times* to inform me that the CSA had huge computer problems .... Said my stock-pot prayer, St Valium pray for me!

My frustration was overcome by a call to what could have been the location for Ken Loach's fine film *Cathy Come Home*, which gave birth to the charity Shelter.

I had received an urgent phone message from one of Worcester's Neighbourhood Offices concerning the re-housing of a mother with three children who had to have emergency accommodation but couldn't take their Labrador. Dave and Donna at the kennels were stars over the re-homing of the pet, which they were not obliged to take as it was not a stray.

I arrived at the family's new home off the Martley Road, which was as spartan as the top of Worcester Beacon, the only warmth being their focus on this fine otter-tailed Labrador. I was greeted as if I were the undertaker, but didn't have to use that most chilling of all professional introductions, 'Hello, where is the deceased?'

All I could find to say was, 'Life is hard', and that uttered as clearly as I could make it without breaking down. The dog was disturbed by all the tears, not knowing they were directed at its ensuing unhappiness. I asked for a letter which would be legal proof that the Labrador was actually in the mother's giving, and did not belong to her ex-husband. She handed me the sad missive and a £10 note to help with its upkeep. I felt like making this contribution myself. As I was given the lead, the children's crying increased, only to be punctuated by a list of the pet's likes and dislikes: 'Likes soft food ... doesn't like cars ... he will go to a good home, won't he?'

I knew about the pain of parting. The worst thing about my unemployment was leaving behind the laughter of children in the walls of our rambling house when we were forced to sell up. To try and soothe their grief, I said, 'This is not about you personally, but this house is marked in the Council books as a centre of barking and fouling. I have previously counted twenty-five sets of faeces in your back yard and so your landlord has got to know about it.'

The two girls slowly followed me out to Pixie with the scant accoutrements of comfort a family can give a dog. They then laid them on the road at the rear of Pixie, placed there in slow motion like a daisy chain put lovingly on a pet's grave. They did not turn to look back. A more eloquent and tender witness against family break-up could hardly be rendered.

Monday 2nd April 2002

Lunchtime relief and amusement in the toilets at the Country-side Park.

Enter two little boys, one about eight and the other perhaps six. They did what they had to do and then the younger one says, 'Can I have a packet of them condoms, please?'

The older, pulling himself up to his full height to exercise his loco parentis, though he was barely higher than the trough, said, 'They are not sweets, yer know!'

The younger nipper twitched his nose while replying, imagining he was being swindled out of a treat by some sophistry. 'So what are they then?' The answer from the little worldling was swift and terse, 'They are to stop ladies having babies!'

'Well,' says junior, 'What happens to the ambulance and the ambulance driver, then?'

Some days start frumpy and try to straighten themselves up later. This day ended up with a certain tug on my sleeve.

My dog phone rang while I was trying to shove a restive Fox Hound, possibly loose from the Fernhill Heath pack, into Pixie's cage. It was Magie saying that a Civil Service call centre in Scotland had phoned up offering me a job in the Department of Work! (sic) and Pensions in Birmingham. As a hungry dog is easily biddable, I rang up immediately and accepted without even asking about terms. Today, seemingly, someone pressed the right computer button to end my professional exile and disintegration.

The deliberate policy of unemployment, this bogle in the vestry of the nation, is the manipulation of madness. But the chaos of it all, for me, is now at an end. I existed in a static state where there was neither fulfilment nor frustration and, in order to make do, everything had to be botched with a fragile dignity. Nevertheless, being nearer to sixty than to fifty years of age, I do have to attempt to re-invent myself as an old monkey keen to learn new faces.

The only times when age should really matter are to do with wine and cheese.

So, my doormat finally wears its bristles with pride for a job well done as it prepares to receive my letter of engagement from the Civil Service. As always, doormat endures sun and rain alike or whatever else falls from above. It does not suffer from the weakness of irascible ambition, so as it aspires to nothing, nothing has any power over it. Doormat is never really disheartened and remains to this day where I put it and is content to be there and to stay there in its place.

Worcester Woman

This just leaves me with the delectable task of choosing my Worcester Woman from my list of worthies, for which I need to consider not just their beauty but discreet charisma too. Some had been broken on the rack of life, in situations where tribulation did not easily present itself as a spur to action, while others were so favourably portfolioed, they were assured of preferment over lesser mortals.

Over my three-year tenure, I had half considered awarding it jointly to Natasha and the children's canine confraternity of Tolladine, by virtue of their freshness and for their love of dogs.

Then of course there was the wondrous Miss Rebecca Madresfield, but she is surely young enough to win it another day and for other reasons, those being for care and loyalty which are of more value than success.

The widow of Elm Green Close whom I recently scrutinised also moved me deeply.

I then recollected all the 'ladies' I had encountered, some staggeringly gorgeous and wildly self-made, like Maria, Simone and Katherine, so obviously prime candidates; but no. Maybe it should go to all my lady colleagues in the office, especially Kate the Good, who struggled sometimes heroically behind the scenes to keep so much filth from tainting the environment and citizens of Worcester.

Besides all the others, I should include Jan Barnes from the Cathedral staff, who on one occasion was as welcome to me as a Co-op bus at a rainy funeral. During a bad day when I was fraught and knocknobbled, dear sensitive Jan took me up the stairs to the nave library and let me handle medieval liturgical texts, which were secreted from Cromwell's destructive eyes. This simple gesture of hers rendered them once again instruments of healing.

Shiny Sixpence, naturally, is in the top ten; so is the anonymous lady who illuminated the darkness of the Cathedral with the renewal of her marriage vows. Emily is not included. Polly is included; so are the literary sisters from The Arboretum. I ought also to say Miss Sixpence has gone to join the ranks of the 'coffin dodgers,' a description which I am sure would make her laugh. She is receiving twenty-four-hour care at her brother's farmhouse and so has now been united permanently with her beloved Collie, Bradley.

As I picked my way through my bevy of beauties, I thought of the generously shaped personage and charitable virtues of WPC Becky Giblin and all the ladies from the front desk at Worcester Police Station with their never-ending coffee cups and much personal kindness.

Then I saw in my mind's eye someone whom surely the dilettante socialists of the Labour Party at Millbank would have overlooked. But then they are not here in Worcester to avail themselves of this person, nor are they regularly in dark frozen fields before the roosters. She is Mary Old, my civic angel, who daily collects all the dog filth in her little white pick-up truck, depositing bags of defecation in the Council yard. Not only this, she also exhibits a care and a provision of time for both the people and the animals of this fine shire city, which goes way above the norms of her contractual position.

Mary, who is guided by the plaintive spirits of little creatures, is my Worcester Woman par excellence

Monday April 22nd 2002

Bade farewell to the sweetness and the spirit of Broadheath Common.

Tuesday 23 April 2002

Magie to the Birmingham University Medical School's Department of Cancer Research for an interview as a secretary. My dear wife has been consigned to the same fate as myself, since she too was forced into job hunting. Doormat has also had to catch pieces of dreary brown paper marked P45 with her name printed on it.

Friday 26th April 2002

Doormat mightily upset again, on Magie's behalf this time. It was the fob-off from Birmingham University. My wife, Anne-Marie, being under the same sentence as myself, is no stranger to the *salon de rejection*, or the yellow-toothed *Chienne du Monde* (Bitch of the world) which jumps on you and never barks. This description of depression and the 'unhappiness that is howling inside you' is so ably rendered by her fellow Breton, Pierre-Jakez Helias, in his chronicle of old Breton life, *The Horse of Pride*. (Yale University Press 1978.)

The first week in May, and my relationship with my wordy yet silent companion, this Diary, is coming to an end.

Final poo patrol, but nothing seen. I took off my uniform more speedily than I had first put it on almost three years ago. And so I drove Pixie Vauxhall to bed, not returning her home to the City Council of Worcester as you might think, but to Paragon Security, the contractor who had engaged me to provide dog services for Worcester.

I had become a beneficiary of privatisation, which I had always considered a dubious financial initiative and an eclipse of civic conscience. Such measures are usually in someone else's financial interest and never your own. An anonymous Worcestershire ditty puts the case against privatisation rather elegantly:

Great is the fault in man or woman
That steals a goose from off a common,
But who can plead that man's excuse
Who steals the common from the goose? (1)

Despite this protest, Paragon did take my safety seriously through the provision of a bodyguard when violence was anticipated or I faced a known nasty canine. But my Worcester world of work had barely enough of that indefinable liquid, the one which oils the wheels of life, to smooth the conflicting demands of a local security company with those of the City Council. Unhappily, Paragon saw me as being integrated into their organisation, which tried to operate within a buccaneering security industry, while Worcester City Council regarded me as their own immutable civic servant.

During my tenure I achieved a high mark on the Index of Canine Actual Clearance Time (aggression adjusted) ICACT. However, in spite of my results, I regretted my failure to replace the betrayal of Worcester's dogs with the norms of responsible ownership. Like a motorway patrolman who deals only with bad drivers, I mostly saw bad dogs, but behind most bad dogs are inadequate owners. Certainly, I will miss the simple service of brightening the forlorn features of one of the wonders of all creation – the dog!

As I leave I ought to state that the worst quadruped I ever came across was not a dog at all but the Nazi Donkey of Pershore! This creature was loaned out for village fetes, but would always throw handicapped children off its back. And whilst on the subject of reckoning, the worst fouler I ever came across was a filly in Bevere. This horse, having been spooked by a passing vehicle, swung its rear around onto the pavement and, in an act of supreme equestrian comedy, deposited a steaming calling card all over a young bullet-headed dog walker and his Golden Labrador.

The pedestrian did not seem immediately to appreciate the instant transformation of his jeans from blue to camouflage motley, though his dog, despite the dripping splatter on its face, seemed to me to compose a huge smile through the slosh in wonder at such munificence.

My wanderings now at an end, I gave thanks to all the people I loved in Farrier House, and really meant it. They had taken me to themselves like an old sofa to a new form. If I did anything in the environmental department, it was because of all of them. No speeches were made but Martin Gillies read out a poem about me. It began:

The hounds of Warndon howled night long,
Their owners did so too,
For they had heard that Bernie
Was to leave for pastures new ....

Then I slipped away, hoping for Byron's 'other and better things even in this life.'

So, I did not say much as I left, as the word is not enough. Nor did I bother to pause and swivel to look back down Farrier Street. Now demobbed, I made this last entry in my diary, a journal which I now see straddles some events around the millennium.

I decided to visit the Cathedral, and noticed this time that the Elgar statue opposite actually looks right past the mystical building, peering beyond and into the future.

Elgar was a frustrated dog lover but towards the end of his life he surrounded himself with several dogs, perhaps as companions because of the loss of his wife, Caroline Alice (who would never allow them through the door):

'In 1932 at the approach of Christmas and not long before Elgar died, he attended a meeting of the old Worcester Glee Club (a gathering for performing short works). Keith Prowse were publishing three of his pieces for piano, *Serenade, Adieu* and *Mina* [named after the smallest of his Cairn Terriers, whose grave, by the side gate at Elgar's Broadheath cottage, Magie and I tend when we visit].

'That year, Elgar's Christmas card bore an original fable. It described a group of angels discussing the Last Judgement without enthusiasm. Lucifer recommended Shakespeare and Milton. But the Maker Of All replied by creating a puppy. Through the ages, Man could be serenely happy with his Dog.' (2)

Thus, the spirit that I found haunting Broadheath Common, the place which was an antidote to 'the paddy' of my own desolation, drew to its earthly close with a touching composition about a favourite dog and a happy reflection about a little puppy.

For me, I swap Broadheath Common for an open plan office, and my place on the parapet of Powick Old Bridge for a workstation, a computer, and an in-tray.

The End, I hope.

If one of my made-up names is the same as that for any living person, this is pure coincidence. Names can be changed by a statutory declaration at a solicitor near you, or by use of a collar and name tag from your local pet shop.

Badger Cartwright, Worcester and Château Chaos, Stourbridge. September 1999 – Easter 2006

(1) *Words Of Old Worcestershire* (Kenneth Tompkinson Ltd 1980)

(2) Quoted in *Edward Elgar – A Creative Life*. Jerrold Northrop Moore (OUP 1987)

Bernard Cartwright lives in Stourbridge and is married, with four grown-up children. He enjoyed many roller-coaster years with I.T.V., firstly as a cameraman, and then as a researcher/director. He than became director of the Churches' Council for Health and Healing, before getting entangled in canine affairs.He now works as a civil servant in Birmingham and enjoys family life with his French wife, Magie.

Photo: by kind permission of *Worcester Evening News*